Feels like I'm Breathing

ANYA McKEE

TORN CURTAIN PUBLISHING
Wellington, New Zealand
www.torncurtainpublishing.com

ISBN Softcover 978-1-991299-38-3
ISBN EPub 978-1-991299-39-0

Cataloguing in Publication Data:
Title: Feels Like I'm Breathing
Author: Anya McKee
Subjects: Cross-cultural living, Turkey, Missions, Christian Living, Biography, Women's Interest, Prayer, Marriage, Spirituality, Personal Growth, Discipleship.

To my precious family

I honor the generations that have gone before me

and bless the generations ahead.

Together we are building a dynasty.

CONTENTS

Preface

She sat beside me, our bare backs leaning against the warm marble wall of the women's hammam. My friend had come all the way from Australia with her husband and four kids, and for a whole week they had poured themselves out, helping our family in a myriad of ways. It was time to take a break and whisk her off for the ultimate tourist experience—an afternoon at the Turkish baths. She was brave, to be honest, because if you're not used to stripping off close to naked and having a good wash, scrub and relaxing lounge-around in the company of strangers, the whole thing can be, to say the least, intimidating.

But she'd agreed, because she was determined to experience the life I was now immersed in—and, I suspect, because she sensed my need to get away from the family awhile and share our hearts, woman-to-woman.

It had been less than a year since we'd left Australia and moved our own family of six across the world to settle in Turkey. We wanted to take our small editing company and see what we could make of it in the Middle Eastern market. But more than that, we wanted the chance to live as a Christian family in a country where most people have never met a Christian or had a Christian friend. With a very simple plan—live in Turkey and follow Jesus, just as we would at home—we went.

But the idea started a year or two before that, and it began when we shifted the way we prayed. Instead of asking God to come and be with us in whatever we were doing, we began to ask if He would open our eyes to what *He* was doing, and if we might have the privilege of joining Him in that. We'd started caring less about what was on our heart, and instead asking Him more about what was on His.

Such a prayer, as you can imagine, led us deeper into a realm we had never given enough consideration to—the unseen realm, the spiritual environment in which we all live. And, more particularly, the heavenlies. The presence of God. If God is Spirit, and we wanted to see what He was doing, we'd need to become familiar with His presence. But that's a story in itself.

The more unexpected result of our prayer was that Turkey started coming up. *Turkey, of all places.* Taxi drivers, news bulletins, people who had invested in Turkey for years . . . it was as if God said, '*You want to join me where I'm at work?*', then took our cheeks lovingly between his hands, and turned our faces toward Turkey.

In the six months between asking God to align our lives with what He was up to, and boarding a plane bound for Istanbul, something astounding happened. In short, God went to work on our family. He was about to position us on a steep learning curve—one that would expand our spiritual experience far beyond where we'd been before.

Jeff and I knew firsthand the stories of those who had gone to difficult countries full of faith, fueled by a clear call and a passion for people, only to return years later in turmoil. Our story, we sensed deep down, needed to be a redemption story; we needed a new paradigm—not just for our sake, but for the generations that would follow—and as God began deliberately ministering into our lives, we found ourselves eager to respond.

Night after night, we'd tuck the children into bed and then start praying—in our determination to go over our lives with a fine-toothed comb, we prayed forgiveness over sins and offenses, we broke curses passed that had been passed down to our generation; we got a grasp on how the enemy takes ground in our lives and communities, and we learned to worship with new levels of abandon. It was a crash-course in Christian spirituality, and as we took it and ran with it, our spiritual confidence grew too.

So it was, that with powerful new perspectives, a rock-solid promise from God of peace and safety for the days ahead, and the heartfelt love and support of an incredible Team of Friends, we boarded a plane in Australia and landed, thirty-three hours later, in Turkey. What we didn't foresee was that, from the moment we hit the ground, we would spend our days simply trying to keep up with what God was doing.

We set up a home in the last city we ever expected to find ourselves in, a city renowned for its history and trade, and the destination of choice for fervently religious Saudi Arabian tourists who would come to pray at the Great Mosque and the tombs of the Sultans. I couldn't have been prouder of the way our family had taken on the whole crazy venture. We settled in quickly, adjusted to pretty much every new experience, and embraced the many unexpected opportunities that came our way. Our website had just been translated into Turkish, which bode well for business, we'd made incredible friends in our neighborhood, and I was leading an unlikely group of expats in the audacious quest to pull off projects that would benefit both the city and the foreigners who lived there.

But now we were six months in. A visit to the Turkish bath was just what I needed, and not just for the chance to relax and soak up the company of a friend from home. Truth is, I'd been on edge for a while now. The pressures of living in Turkey had been relentless. We'd done a stellar job of rising above it all, but the reality was that something was taking its toll. All our strengths were coming out, *but so were all our uglies.* And Jeff and I had started arguing. A lot.

Why was it that every time he spoke, I took him the wrong way? Why was I suddenly so easily provoked by every little thing my husband did? We thought we'd been thorough about dealing with our issues before we left for Turkey. *What, then, was this? How did we get to the point where we were basically avoiding each other?*

Soon we gave up arguing; we were too tired for it anyway. The easier alternative was to put our heads down, get on with life, and interact as little as possible. Of course, we pulled it together for the visitors, for the kids, for the sake of keeping people fed and facilitated,.but the thought had started to fester in my mind . . . I was beginning to believe we might return home one day with an incredible God-story to tell, but no marriage to salvage.

How on earth . . .?

I don't know how it came up, but my friend was comfortable now, the warmth of the room had eased into our muscles, and the steady stream of water pouring from the marble lion's mouth into the pool below muted the conversations taking place around us. She was talking about her marriage, how happy they were now, but how it hadn't always been that way. I managed to keep my poise, my vulnerability-bubble nicely intact, but my ears were tuned to her every word.

'We'd done counselling,' she said, 'but we weren't getting far.'

I have an innate love of hearing people tell how their lives have been transformed, but this time, there was more at stake. This time, I was listening like my life depended on it. 'What changed?' I asked her.

'Well, in the end, it came down to obedience. The Bible says that a wife should love and respect her husband, and I committed to that. I learned to honor him; I chose every day to show him respect. He worked hard at it too. Over time, it made a real difference.'

And it was in that moment, in a twisted sort of way, that I found my answer.

The thing is, I know myself well enough to know that following through with good intentions has never come easily to me. I could make up my mind to be a better wife to Jeff. I could tell myself, '*the Bible says it; therefore, I'll do it,*' but the reality was, I could hardly sustain the good intention to read my children a bedtime story every night. There's something about committing to *every*. *Every morning. Every day. Every time he . . . Every time I . . .* The truth is, after years of trying, I didn't trust myself to sustain the effort. I was tired just thinking about the level of intent it would take to reshape my thoughts, my responses for the long haul. But there was something deeper that fueled my dissatisfaction with what I'd just heard.

You see, I wasn't looking for an 'Anya-tried-harder' story. I'd tried. I'd failed. Now, I was looking for a God-story. I *needed* a God-story. In fact, I wanted a *God-changed-everything* story. I wasn't here on the other side of the world to show people how awesome I was. I was here to show them how awesome Jesus is. How He transforms lives. Only, the life that needed transformation in this moment, was mine. Thankfully, my friend had given me what I needed. Through her, my moment of clarity had come. *I wouldn't do anything to fix our marriage. Nothing.* No *'Good morning darling.'* No *'how was your day?'* No, *'I think you're doing an incredible job.'* No sex.

In my raw desperation, I decided that if this were to really be a God-story, then He could do it all. I would submit to God—that was fine—and if *He* told me to say something, or do something, I would, without hesitation. But I would do nothing on my own initiative. This thing needed fixing right at the foundation, and I wasn't about to build on a mess of my own making.

Two things happened in the month that followed.

The first was that a friend loaned me their copy of a book called *'Captivating.'* John and Stasi Eldredge had written about the beauty of a woman's soul. I had heard many stories of women who had been impacted by that book; I had actually started reading it several years earlier but not even made it to the end—despite the rave reviews my friends were giving, nothing in the book seemed to connect with me.

This time it was a whole different story. But now I had come a long way in my personal journey. I was hungry, desperate, teachable, and I had gained a healthy appreciation that evil was real, that there was more to the battle for our souls than meets the eye. On one level, Jeff and I both knew that we were not really each other's ene-my—that there was an enemy outside ourselves, who was scheming right from the start to destroy us. The issue was, we weren't getting much in the way of victory. On top of that, I had begun to despise myself. This time, I read the entire book in one night.

At end was a prayer. Now, written prayers had never been a big part of my world, but as I read through this Daily Prayer for Freedom, I came across phrases and concepts that were unfamiliar to me, and yet, they had a clear ring of truth to them. I sensed this was exactly what I needed to pray if I were to get some level of breakthrough in our marriage.

The second thing that happened that month, was that Ramadan began. In Turkey, Ramadan affects everything, not the least, the way the day begins. We were used to waking to the sound of the call to prayer as it moved from East to West across our city, simultane-ously blaring from the multitude of minarets that surrounded our apartment. But now it was Ramadan, and our first introduction to the month of fasting was being woken at four a.m. by enthusiastic young men as they ran up and down the pitch-black streets of the city, beating great Ottoman-style drums, calling the faithful to rise and eat before the call to prayer rang out, the sun came up, and the long day of fasting commenced.

I decided I would rise with the beating of the drums. If the locals could get out of bed at four a.m., I could too.

And so it was that on the first day of Ramadan, I eased myself out of bed, tiptoed in the predawn darkness down three flights of marble stairs, knelt down on an old Turkish rug, and began speaking out some of the most powerful words I have ever used.

'Lord, I close my ears and mind to any voice that is not Yours. I shut out every distracting voice, every voice of the enemy, even my own scrambled thoughts, and I choose to listen to Your Holy Spirit alone.'

Every morning, as the family slept, I poured out my soul to God. And I wrote. I wrote every word I said to God, and every word He said to me. It turns out I didn't need the whole month of Ramadan. Three weeks in, I had my God-story. . .

DAILY PRAYER FOR FREEDOM

(A PRAYER OF JOHN AND STASI ELDREDGE)

My dear Lord Jesus, I come to you now to be restored in You—to renew my place in You, my allegiance to You, and to receive from You all the grace and mercy I so desperately need this day. I honor You as my sovereign Lord and surrender every aspect of my life totally and completely to You. I give You my body as a living sacrifice; I give You my heart, soul, mind, and strength; and I give You my spirit as well. I cover myself with Your blood—my spirit, my soul, and my body. And I ask Your Holy Spirit to restore my union with You, seal me in You, and guide me in this time of prayer.

Dear God, holy and victorious Trinity, You alone are worthy of all my worship, my heart's devotion, all my praise and all my trust and all the glory of my life. I worship You, bow to You, and give myself over to You in my heart's search for life. You alone are Life, and You have become my life. I renounce all other gods, all idols, and give You the place in my life that You truly deserve. I confess here and now that it is all about You, God, and not about me. You are the Hero of this story, and I belong to You. Forgive me for my every sin. Search me and know me and reveal to me any aspect of my life that is not pleasing to You, expose any agreements I have made with my enemy, and grant me the grace of a deep and true repentance.

Heavenly Father, thank you for loving me and choosing me before You made the world. You are my true Father—my Creator, my Redeemer, my Sustainer, and the true end of all things, including my life. I love You; I trust You; I worship You. Thank you for proving

Your love for me by sending your only Son, Jesus, to be my sacrifice and new life. I receive Him and all His life and all His work, which You ordained for me. Thank you for including me in Christ, for forgiving me my sins, for granting me His righteousness, for making me complete in Him. Thank you for making me alive with Christ, raising me with Him, seating me with Him at Your right hand, granting me His authority, and anointing me with the Holy Spirit. I receive it all with thanks and give it total claim to my life.

Jesus thank you for coming for me, for ransoming me with Your own life. I honor You as my Lord. I love You, worship You, trust You. I sincerely receive You as my redemption, and I receive all the work and the triumph of Your crucifixion, whereby I am cleansed from all sin through Your shed blood, my old nature is removed, my heart is circumcised unto God, and every claim being made against me is disarmed. I take my place in Your cross and death, whereby I have died with You to sin, and to the world, and to the Evil One. I am crucified with Christ, and I have crucified my flesh with all its passions and desires. I now take up my cross and crucify my flesh with all its pride, unbelief, and idolatry. I put off the old man. I now bring the cross of Christ between me and all people, all spirits, all things. Holy Spirit, apply to me the fullness of the work of the crucifixion of Jesus Christ for me. I receive it with thanks and give it total claim to my life.

Holy Spirit, I sincerely receive You as my Counsellor, my Comforter, my Strength and my Guide. Thank you for sealing me in Christ. I honor You as my Lord, and I ask You to lead me into all truth, anoint me for all my life and walk and calling, and lead me deeper into Jesus today. I fully open my life to You in every dimension and aspect—my body, my soul, and my spirit—choosing to be filled with You, to walk in step with You in all things. Apply to me, blessed Holy Spirit, all of the work and all of the gifts in Pentecost. Fill me afresh, blessed Holy Spirit. I receive You with thanks and give You total claim to my life.

Heavenly Father, thank you for granting to me every spiritual blessing in the heavenlies in Christ Jesus. I receive those blessings into my life today, and I ask the Holy Spirit to bring all those blessings into my life this day. Thank you for the blood of Jesus. Wash me once more with his blood from every sin and stain and evil device. I put on your armor—the belt of truth, the breastplate of righteousness, the shoes of readiness of the gospel of peace, the helmet of salvation. I take up the shield of faith and the sword of the Spirit, the Word of God, and I wield these weapons against the Evil One in the power of God. I choose to pray at all times in the Spirit, to be strong in You, Lord, and in Your might.

Father, thank you for Your angels. I summon them in the authority of Jesus Christ and release them for war for me and my household. May they guard me at all times this day. Thank you for those who pray for me; I confess I need their prayers, and I ask you to send forth your Spirit and rouse them, unite them, raising up the full canopy of prayer and intercession for me. I call forth the Kingdom of the Lord Jesus Christ this day throughout my home, my family, my life, and my domain. I pray all of this in the name of Jesus Christ, with all the glory and honor and thanks to him.[1]

---

1 https://ransomedheart.com/prayer/daily-prayer

PART ONE

Day 1

Lord, you have been so kind to me. Anyone else would have given up long ago. I see it now. I've been silently asking one question. *'Am I worth it? Do I have any real value? Any worth?'* and I keep hearing a resounding *'No!'*

This book, 'Captivating' has got me thinking. *Does anyone think I'm beautiful? Have I ever been lovingly, relentlessly pursued? Can anyone see beyond the sin and ugliness and hatefulness in me? Does anyone care enough to fight for me . . . to walk me through healing until I'm sorted? Is there even one person who sees what You created me to be?*

Dear God, I've looked to others, especially Jeff, to answer the sad questions of my heart and it's left me even more wounded. More vulnerable and troubled. So today I look to You. It's hard to look into Your eyes. In fact, it's hard for me to look at *anyone's* eyes if there's even the slightest chance they might make me feel loved or precious.

Forgive me, God, for taking my insecurities to people—especially to Jeff. My brokenness and pain, my sadness—

it's too much to put onto anyone else. You alone hold the answer. I need You to heal me.

Will You fight for me, Lord? I love You for what You did at Calvary. It's no small thing that You bore my sin away. No small thing at all. But the brokenness? The wounds? The diseases that eat away at my mind, my spirit, even my body? Will You fight for me until my redemption is complete? Until I am restored and whole and the woman You intended me to be? Is there a chance I could experience the sort of abundant life You promise?

I had my Bible open on the floor beside me to Psalm 55. Now, slowly and quietly, I began to read.

As for me, I will call upon God, and the Lord shall save me. Evening and morning and at noon I will pray and cry aloud, and He shall hear my voice. Psalm 55:16

Lord, thank you for Ramadan. I can't believe I'm saying that. But I need this time. If the people around me are getting out of bed to pray for forty days straight, so will I. I will pray this Daily Prayer every morning, and I'll be sure to speak it out loud. I want every being in the spirit-realm, both good and evil, to know that I'm looking to You alone for deliverance and healing and cleansing.

As I read Psalm 55, one verse stood out from among the others, as if the Holy Spirit was highlighting it just for me. I needed to take that verse and make it my prayer.

HE HAS REDEEMED MY SOUL IN PEACE FROM THE BATTLE THAT WAS AGAINST ME. PSALM 55: 18

Father, it's as if my soul is at war with itself. As if one part of me is fighting against the real me, and all I crave is peace within. But this verse is written as if the battle against me is already won. How can I say this when it's not true? Right now, I'm sinking, Lord. My flesh—the stubborn, angsty inner-self—is so strong, and the devil seems to have the upper hand. But I know that if I speak these words on earth, they will meet with a resounding AMEN in Your presence. So here goes . . .

I felt like a phony at first, speaking this verse over my life as if it were a done deal. After all, my soul was far from being at peace. But that's faith. Faith is more than believing. Faith requires speaking out what is meant to be, before there is any hint of the reality. For me, speaking out loud was a hurdle I had to get over. I had become so accustomed to speaking out of hopelessness that words of promise and hope sounded strange on my lips. But it was time to bring my words and my thoughts into alignment with God's. It was time to speak out loud, in faith . . .

I declare ahead of the fact, God, in agreement with You, that this verse is true for me. You (*no one else*) have redeemed (*in the nick of time, I suspect*) my soul (*the very essence of me, which now lies trampled and broken*), in peace (*I can only imagine*), from the battle that was against me.

Oh God. It's a battle all right. Only I've failed to fight, and it appears You are the only one wielding a sword for me.

For me, Lord? This isn't some battle for territory or for the masses, is it? It's personal. When You fight for me, I can imagine believing that maybe You find me worth it. It's as if I hear a faint whisper of a *'yes'* to my question already! That's very kind of you, Lord.

Thank you.

Oh, and Lord, there's one more phrase I forgot to include:

. . . FOR THERE WERE MANY AGAINST ME. PSALM 55:18

Lord, I realize this could take a while. I've had thirty-seven years so far, and I imagine the number of hurts, sins, accusations, heartaches, wounds . . . I suspect they vastly outnumber the years of my life. Though I don't know which enemy to turn on first, it's reassuring to hear You acknowledge how many there are, and still to know You'll do this for me. Are You sure I'm worth the trouble? When we're finally done, will there be any time left to enjoy the new me?

So far, that first morning, I had brought my heart to God, and I'd found my thoughts guided by His Word. Now, his response came to me even more personally. As I lingered in His presence, I heard Him speak.

> *Anya, there will be Eternity to enjoy you.*
> *I'll keep fighting for you until we face the very last enemy—death.*

In this life, I'll never cease fighting for you.

Thank you, Lord! That sounds a lot like love.

Day 2

I began the next morning with the same prayer. *My dear Lord Jesus, I come to You now to be restored in You . . .'* I was taking it slowly. I needed the Holy Spirit to lead me, even as I prayed. Right up front I found myself pausing at these words: '. . . reveal any aspect of my life that is not pleasing to You. *Expose any agreements I have made with my enemy* and grant me the grace of a deep and true repentance.'

'Expose any agreements I have made with my enemy.'

Lord, my mind is going back to when Jeff first asked me if I would go out with him.

We were sitting on the back stairs of my house. We'd been chatting about all sorts of things, when the conversation took a turn, and Jeff came out with the life-altering words, *'Anya, would you like to go out with me?'* Part of me was thrilled, of course. I wanted to blurt out, 'Really?! I'd love to!' and to follow it up with a happy dance. Instead, another voice in me responded and I found myself answering, 'Really, Jeff? You don't want me. I'm not worth it. Believe me. I'll break your heart.'

8

Oh God! What kind of twisted thing was that, that happened in my mind? Even then, I knew I would be hard work, that I'd disappoint him. In fact, I think I believed deep down not just that I would disappoint him, but that *I was disappointing.* So, I rejected his simple, *'I want you'* and threw it back at him. No doubt the Enemy was quick to heartily agree with my words. But God, that was where I was at. Consumed with myself and my unworthiness. What should I do?

Renounce those words, Anya. Send them back to where they came from.

Okay. I'll give this a go.

In Jesus' name, I renounce the words I spoke to Jeff that he didn't really want me, that I would break his heart and that I wasn't worth it. I annul those words and the thought that backed them up, that *I am a disappointment*, and in Jesus name, I break my agreement with the enemy. I declare that the Enemy may never utter or use those words *to me*, or *about me*, or against Jeff and I and our marriage.

At this point, a thought came into my mind. If, when Jeff asked me to go out with him, I had been aware of the unseen realm around us, how would my response have been different? I sensed that an unkind voice had whispered in my ear—that Satan wanted to get a foothold in our relationship right from the start. But where was God? What if I had been aware of Him in that moment? If I had been tuned in to Him? And so, I asked . . .

Dear Lord, can we go back to that scene? You were present,

overhearing this foolish response spoken from my very own lips. *What was I thinking?* But more to the point, what were *You* thinking? I want You to take me back there, Lord, maybe even to undo this mess. Can we do that now, Lord? Can we go back to the steps of my house in Brisbane and fix the whole thing up from the start? You are outside of time. Can we go back and re-run that whole scene?

Yes, let's do that.

Picture me, Anya. I am right here with you both. I've seen Jeff summon his courage and bare his heart to you. I'm proud of that young man.

Now Anya, wait! Before you answer, step aside with Me for a minute! This is a significant and sacred moment. Let me help you grasp the joy right now. Anya—he wants you! Your mind is swirling, and if you grab a random thought, it may not be true. Shut your ears to the Liar and listen to Me. You need to trust Me when I say this: You are my daughter, and you will make Jeff very happy. You will help him, you'll complete him. You don't break things, Anya, least of all, hearts. In fact, you'll get to bind up his heart. It's okay for him to want you. It's okay to give yourself to him. Why don't you promise to do him good, and not evil, all the days of your life?

Okay, Lord.

As my husband and children slept upstairs, I simply spoke out my revised answer to the question Jeff had asked me twenty years earlier. In the spirit, I came back to that scene, looked up at Jeff and gave him the answer he had longed for. *'Yes, Jeff! Yay! I'd love to go out with you!'*

Anya, that's good. But I want you to do more than revise your history. I want us to address an earlier scenario in your life—the moment that set you up to answer Jeff like that in the first place.

Lord, I'm remembering when our church put on a farewell afternoon tea for my family, right before we left for Albania. I remember all the people who had expressed their concern to mum and dad about going—about how it would impact us, their four children. None of it was positive or faith-filled, but the words that particularly stayed with me were from an old man. Lord, I was only seventeen at the time, had just said goodbye to all my friends and future as I knew it, and then I overheard him give a parting comment to my parents. *'That's the one you need to watch,'* he said, pointing at me. *'She'll break your hearts.'*

Lord, that memory still hurts, and I don't know why. It was such a throw-away comment, but it really stuck. I thought I'd forgiven him. Are You saying it hasn't worked? Why are You bringing it up again?

Anya. You are hurt and I wanted to show you where it all started. I'm teaching you how to break the hold these things have over you. To live without offense. You need to go back there. When that man said you'd break your parents heart and that you'd disappoint them, that cut deep, didn't it? Yes, it was a careless comment, but it inflicted a wound that has festered for years, and the Enemy took advantage of that the moment Jeff asked you out.

Those words didn't come from me, Anya. You don't hurt people. Quite the opposite. I reject the words that man spoke. You should reject them too. Don't respond to Jeff out of a wounded heart.

Thank you, Lord. In Jesus' name, I now annul the words spoken over me by that man; I renounce the lie that I have broken my parents' heart, and I renounce the lie that I will break Jeff's heart too. I cut off my words and break my agreement with the Enemy in Jesus' name.

Now to finish this off, Anya, you need to forgive. I want to teach you something.

I had only ever known to forgive by getting face to face with those who had hurt me, or by privately telling the Lord I forgave them. But I'd always wondered. *Was I genuine? Did I really mean it? Was my forgiveness adequate?* I'd done my best, but I still found myself mulling over sad old memories or responding out of hurt more often than not. I needed something more than what I could muster. Something beyond myself.

I was being summoned into the heavenlies—into the presence of God. I had always loved reading about the moment during Jesus' death when the great curtain that hung in the temple was torn. It signified that a way had been made for humanity to be restored to God. But now it was not just a moment in history. Now I was being invited to make the most of that momentous event, to respond to heaven's open invitation and come on in. This felt new, but my spirit was willing. Tentatively, I clenched the edge of the curtain in my hand, peeked through to what lay on the other side, cast a look back over my shoulder at this world, and then slipped into Zion. My heavenly home.

And there it was—a *river* of forgiveness, a mighty torrent, a river in the heavenlies that gushes and flows and never runs dry; an endless supply that Jesus unleashed on the cross, sufficient to wash away every hurt, every offense, every sin. Now I saw it. My own ability to forgive was limited, but *His was not*! It was time for me to take my place as a native of both realms, and *pour out heaven's forgiveness* for all the ways I had been hurt.

It was easier than I imagined. I had just got sight of a powerful, plentiful, spiritual resource, and having all this forgiveness at my disposal was more than a relief. I sensed this could even be fun! I pictured taking a great big bucket in my hands and stooped down...

In Jesus' name, I take a great measure of forgiveness and I bring it to the old man who said I would break my parents' hearts. Lord, I wash that scene outside our church with Your forgiveness. I take from Your endless supply and pour it out over him and his words. I release him into Your forgiveness and into mine. In Jesus' name I say the enemy has no power to use his words against me anymore.

One more thing, Anya.

You were scared to place yourself under this son of mine, but there's also an ugly side to that scene with Jeff. You were scared and hurt —but your response that day was also proud and arrogant. You didn't make that moment about Jeff, or even about you as a couple. You made it all about yourself.

I was there, poised to bless you both. I wanted to join you together with humility and kindness. But you weren't familiar with my heart for you. Satan's lies were familiar to you. He's told you again and again that you're not worth loving, and you have played along. When will you listen to me? You need to take forgiveness for yourself.

Yes, Lord. I come again into Your presence and stoop down for a fresh measure of forgiveness for myself. I wash myself in Your forgiveness; I bathe in it, Lord. You're right. I have functioned out of my woundedness and in so doing I have wounded others. Please forgive me for speaking those words to Jeff—words full of distrust and selfishness. Today I take forgiveness for what I said back then, and for the consequences we have lived with through the years. I declare the power of those words is broken now, in Jesus name.

Day 3

Lord, it was so good to have some girlfriends over this morning. They're always great company. But can I ask about the yearnings that their visit stirred up in me? You saw me, Lord—I scrambled around before they arrived to get the house straightened and tidy, but inside, I was upset. The whole place was a mess, and all I could think was what a huge job it is to recover from a shambles, and how that feels like my whole life right now. I did what I could, but there was no time to vacuum the floors or clean the bathrooms, and all I could do with the children's rooms was to close the doors.

Lord, it feels like this has less to do with wanting to impress and more about longing for everything to *just stay lovely*. The way it gets to me is out of proportion with reality. My goodness, Lord, we're a family. *Of course* we make a mess. But I feel so uptight about it. Like I just can't let it go. Lord, can you heal me? I feel like I'm grieving.

This isn't just about a house that I constantly need to get back in order—it's about all the things that cannot be recovered. It's our life back home in Australia, and the hand stitched quilt I gave away, it's the years I can't get back with my sister and her kids. And it's me. I constantly deal with my issues, the clutter in my head and heart, only to find that down the track, I'm a mess again. Like housework that won't stay done.

It feels like a conspiracy against anything of beauty or value, and I find myself getting angry at others. The person who forgot a placemat and left a heat stain on our lovely oval dining table. Whoever it was who packed my collection of Christmas books that now seem to have disappeared. The child who dropped the fine china teacup I carefully packed and transported by hand all the way across the world . . .

Lord, I've blamed the ones I love, but they're not really at fault, are they? Is this how the enemy works? Making things look like an accident or neglect? Setting people up for blame, when it's his doing all along?

> *Of course. He hates beauty. He once was beautiful himself; he shared my beautiful home. Now he goes after it. He is the destroyer. He opposes loveliness. He diminishes value.*

Oh, God . . . I bring this wound to You. Today I just wished I had a nice tea set to use with my friends. That's all. What do I do?

> *Let's start with some shifting of your angst to the right place. Repent of the times you've focused your blame on your family. They feel bad about it all too.*

Lord Jesus, I confess I have been accusing my own family. 'You break everything;' 'can't you look after anything?' Mean words, too, like, 'none of you care,' and hopeless words like, 'why even bother?' Lord, I've stood right alongside the devil, hurling accusations. I'm so, so sorry. In Jesus' precious name I cut off those statements once and for all.

I declare that my family was created to express God's heart for beauty and preservation; not for chaos and destruction. And I take back my words that I don't care anymore. I do. Satan, you have lied to me and right now, I expose your lies. My family are not the enemy. My beautiful things *do* matter. I matter. In the end, you're the enemy of my *soul*. But hear this. Jesus is the Lover of my soul. Jesus loves *me*.

> *Now, put an end to this run of 'accidents.' Forbid him to touch your lovely things. Forbid him to mess with your home. Resist Him, Anya.*

I take my stand in Jesus, against the Enemy. Satan, I forbid loss and destruction and I declare you may not rob me and my family of our dignity. Jesus makes all things beautiful. Jesus is all desirable. Jesus is in this home.

Right then a huge wave of sadness came over me. I had a sudden flood of memories—all the things I'd had over the years that were important or precious to me that had somehow been lost along the way. My childhood collection of teaspoons, the many stories I'd written through my teenage years, keepsakes from school days and travel, even the friendships I hadn't been able to cultivate as we'd moved around the world. These were the things that made my life feel rich and beautiful, and I suddenly felt I had very little to show for it all.

Dear child, we've only touched the surface of this beauty issue. We've got some deep, hefty roots to dig up. We need to forgive a lot of people and a lot of situations. We need to heal wounds. We need to acknowledge your many, many losses. A lot of that loss was not of your doing. You valued things that others may not have considered important, and you've taken this very personally. May I take it personally for you instead?

God, this beauty issue could take a lifetime. We've only talked about *things*, and already the hurt and sadness feels unbearable. What about *my* lost beauty? When did that get so mangled? I look in the mirror and I feel ugly. I'm so far from what You created that it's nearly unthinkable that I'll even be restored. Whatever's going on in my spirit has taken its toll on my body. It shows on my face. Can that ever be reversed?

Anya, we need to take it slowly. Remember that old lady you saw, up in the mountains the other day? Her head was covered in an old scarf, she wore faded clothes, and she was alone. But, Anya, she had a posy of wildflowers in her hand. She had searched for beauty even there on that scraggly mountain, amidst all that dust and overgrown grass and rocks. She'd taken a handful of beauty for herself.

She saw you looking at her; heard you quiet whisper, 'çok guzel,' 'so beautiful.' And in that moment, two women I love shared beauty with one another. That's how it should be. I watched you look for some flowers too. In fact, you were so focused on finding wildflowers that you ended up a bit lost. But you found your way back with a stash of your own, and it made me smile.

But Anya, some of those flowers fell to the ground. Kids ran over the top of them, others wilted—they weren't designed to last the hot journey home. It's okay. I want you to know there is beauty everywhere. Sometimes it's for keeping; other beauty is for the moment, for noticing, for turning your heart to me; for awakening your spirit.

You don't need to hoard beauty. You need to notice it.

And one last thing. I know how this feels. I left the beauty of my home too. I too, know what it is like to have no beauty in the eyes of others. I love you.

Day 4

Well, Lord. This battle isn't going so well is it? Why did I even think about beauty? It's a joke. I'm as messed up as they come, inside and out. I hope You don't take that personally; after all, You made me, and I do acknowledge that all You do is so very good.

You must be so disappointed in me. I'm not even a slight reflection of You. If everyone is made in the image of God, what happened? When did I . . . *die*? I used to love life. I sang, I smiled, I dreamed and created and loved. *But now?* I feel like my whole spirit is dying slowly and painfully. When I am alone with You, some part of me is at peace. When I worship You, it feels more real than ever. Your words to me are dearer than anything right now.

But then? Then I go back to my precious family, or into my home—and heaviness takes over. I become ugly in my words, my expressions. I feel dead inside. I hurt the ones I love the most. I feel so incredibly alone. I hate to say it, but I hate myself—how I look, how I feel, how I respond, how I *don't* respond.

Oh Lord. Why should such a wonderful husband get such a pathetic wife? Why make *him* live with such brokenness? Why should these incredible children, so full of potential, so full of wit and intelligence and depth—why should they have to be held back and subjected to me? Why should they have to live with such a dysfunctional, disappointing mother?

If You won't heal me for my sake, Lord, if I'm just not worth it, will You at least heal me for my family's sake? Would You do at least enough so that they don't suffer because of me?

Anya, You want me to heal you. You want me to heal your family, your marriage . . . and you don't want to do it through your efforts, in case it doesn't last. You want to be able to truly say, 'God healed me,' and 'the Lord healed our marriage.' You know your own efforts come to nothing in the end. That you don't have what it takes.

But I'd like to heal you and your delightful family, and I'd like you to join me in the healing. We need to slow down. You need to stay very near to me.

Worship me. I love when you get up early and bow before me, I loved seeing you dance to that beautiful music, all alone last night. That's so you! I love when you pray for freedom and deliverance. Keep drawing near. Listen to my voice. Respond to my promptings. You don't need to follow anyone's formula, or take your own initiative. But when I lead you, or nudge you, or place some action on your heart, I want you to respond, to be brave, to deny yourself even when pride is at stake, and to hold my hand all the way.

I will heal you. I will heal the brokenness in your home. But I do not want you to be idly standing by. We'll do this together, and if we do it my way, it will not be a quick physical solution to cover up a deep spiritual problem. No. We'll sort it all from the roots up.

The nice thing is that, this way, you will find yourself becoming intimate with me, becoming one with Us! So begin with worship. And I know you feel too unworthy and stained and dirty for that. So start by loving me for my sufferings. Take my death for yourself. There's never-ending forgiveness even for you.

Day 5

The next morning, as I prayed the Daily Prayer for Freedom, my very words seemed to mock me. I was reminded of the software that had come pre-installed on my brand-new Turkish laptop. *Unofficial. Replicated. Illegal.*

Dear Lord. When I pray every word of that prayer out loud, I feel like a hypocrite. It's like the little pop-up message on my laptop: *This copy of Windows is not genuine.* I pray, 'my old nature is removed . . . I have crucified my flesh with all its passions and desires' and I hear a voice saying, *'this copy of Anya is not genuine.'* I'm just a fake, Lord, hugely susceptible to viruses and dysfunction—a cheap copy of the real me.

All I can do is keep praying these words to You in the hope that one day you will cause them to be true of me. Until then, thank you for what You're doing in my life.

Day 6

By now, the Ramadan drummer was getting on our nerves. The tension in the community was rising too. People wanted to be devout, but the long hot days with no food or water were taking their toll. At the markets and on the buses, tempers were short. As Christians, we wanted to devote ourselves to praying for the people around us, but the reality was, we were feeling the oppression, our own fuses were short, and the more I prayed, the more the enemy seemed to tighten his grip on my mind. I found myself giving up on ever having a great marriage again.

God, people have talked about having no-one left but You. I've never really known that kind of abandoned feeling until now. It's as if Jeff lives his life so comfortably, so easily—like it doesn't matter to him at all whether I acknowledge him or not. When did I become so insignificant to him? When did this despising start? Has he ever actually loved me?

God, I can't stop these tears. They shake my body and flood my soul. Was I created for this?

He left tonight before dinner with barely a word. Just a token kiss on the head. He came home when he found his class tonight had been cancelled, only to leave again ten minutes later. He loves those students he teaches, Lord. He comes alive around them. Lord, what do they offer that I don't?

Everything, Anya. They offer friendship, admiration, affirmation . . .

Lord, of course I can offer him all that, and more. But he doesn't want me, does he? I guess he's had thirteen years to work out I can't satisfy him in any way at all. Why did You prompt me to deal with those strongholds? Why bother? It feels like I mean nothing to him. Yet he would never leave this marriage. So what do I do? Live the rest of my life in a strained marriage feeling isolated and rejected? Or call it quits and be *that* wife. The one who walked away. Whatever happens, he stays squeaky clean and, in my ugliness of heart, I resent even that.

Well, truth is, he's a lot cleaner and holier and more noble than I, and he deserves better. I'm hopeless, Lord. I've been telling myself that for a long time. I'm too screwed up, and I don't know anyone on this planet who can journey with me into wholeness. Not one person knows how dark it feels inside right now. So what should I expect?

Lord, I am so thankful to You that You encouraged Jeff to fast and pray for our family. But even that left me devastated. God, You saw it. He came home after a long prayer-walk, sat at the other end of the couch, and after barely communicating with me all week, started bringing up past regrets. I know he was sorry for the things he mentioned, but honestly? Did he think that was easy for me to hear? God, he rattled off one scenario after another, muttered *please forgive me*, and moved on. Like he was crossing tasks off his to-do list. God, it half killed me. Does he not think those memories hurt me too? Doesn't he know our marriage is on the line? Why did that have to be all about him? *Him* getting free of it. *Him* finding forgiveness so he can move forward. He didn't want to take me with him on that healing path, Lord, and it hurts.

God, is *this* Your way? Do I just choose to forgive and it's all behind us? I *loved* him, God. I still do. But now I realize I've never really bared my soul to him. I haven't been known the way I long to be known. I've been a fool. He needed someone with no baggage.

> *I'm telling you again. I brought you together. You didn't wrong Jeff by marrying him.*

But I've wronged him ever since, haven't I? I don't know how to be a wife. I don't have a clue how to be a lover to Jeff. And I don't know what to do with all his apologizing.

> *That really got to you, Anya. I know. Satan turns even healing into destruction.*

Well, how can we ever do better? How could that couch-thing have looked any different? It came across so impersonal.

> *Anya, it's okay. Yes, he was simply trying to get the job done. That wasn't*

my style, perhaps, but he was following my lead. I know he made it all about him and I know it went badly. That's why, in this process, you need to get every cue from me. Stay close. But don't minimize this: he apologized to you, Anya. He's sorry. Don't discount the humility or the genuineness of his repentance. There's power in repentance.

Lord, Your heart is so large. So unselfish.

We just imagined we'd have a wonderful marriage, and now I think back over all those days and weeks of harboring our private hurts and misunderstandings, presuming the worst of one another, and there's no way to turn back time and do it differently. It's just so sad, God. My heart breaks for my children. They need to know their Mum and Dad love each other. What on earth are we setting them up for?

*Anya. You have identified so many roots of bitterness—so many wounds in your marriage. You're trying to deal with them, but they are **in your marriage**. Some wounds are shared—and some, you have inflicted on each other. You'll need to be healed of those wounds together. Don't deal with any more unless I tell you.*

Day 7

Father. It's eleven-thirty p.m. I'm alone again. *In Turkey, God.* Jeff went for a walk. Evie is crying in her sleep. Liberty fell out of bed and took ages to settle. The boys haven't responded to me at all today and Jeff seems to have given up. I've cleaned up after dinner and all I'm left with is the feeling I'm no more than a housekeeper and nanny.

> *Anya. Stop now. Do not judge, least you too be judged. Evie was right today when she said Satan was whispering in your ear. He's whispering all sorts of confusing and conflicting thoughts into Jeff's mind too. These are not easy days.*

God, we haven't talked properly for *weeks*. What do I do? I don't trust myself. If I start talking, I'm scared I will mess it up. What if all the pain and hurt and anger comes out as an ugly mess, and we can't deal with it? Oh Lord, when I tried to broach a conversation, Jeff said he was 'waiting for me to snap out of it.'

Oh God, his words hurt. How do I snap out of a life time of ugliness? Of disrespect? Of fear and shame?

I can't bear to look at him. If he so much as glanced into my eyes right now, I think I would break down and sob. Which I can do with You—but with *him*? I don't know if I can be that vulnerable. I don't feel like he cares, and I don't trust myself not to hurt him more.

I'll draw near to him, Anya. I love him too. I love you both.

Day 8

I had just finished listening to a sermon online, and as I sat and took it in, I could feel the hardness in me begin to melt away . . .

Dear Lord, thank you for helping me, thank you for leading me to listen to that sermon about You, Jesus. It means the world that You saw my redemption through to the very end. Your resoluteness, your determination to finish the work of saving me . . . I love you for what you did, even when I was dead towards you. I think of you dying for me and I can nearly hear you say the words I long to hear—*you are worth it.*

I determined to press in closer. I was getting tired, emotionally and physically, but the sermon had stirred something in me, and I found myself with a fresh desire to get the breakthrough that God intended for me. But I needed to know how to proceed . . .

Lord, I'm back. I don't have a clue where to go next. What's on Your mind?

Anya, I want you to take a moment to list all the dreams, the ideals, the potential you see here in Turkey, if only you and Jeff were the truly unified, complimentary team I purposed you to be.

For about half an hour, thoughts flowed. We could worship together and push back the darkness that covers so much of this land. We could start an international church—something our city desperately needed. I imagined prayer-walking together, going out for fun times with other couples, fighting together for the wellbeing of our children, being an amazing role model to the other expat families, having a happy home to invite people to—a home where people felt loved and nurtured and ministered to.

I pictured collaborating together about ways to work together on projects, ways we could share our gifts, our creativity, our writing, art, music and beauty with the world. I wrote a list about exploring new places, getting out of town for a while, getting on top of finances and schooling and all the other pressures.

I imagined raising our children to know that, no matter where they live, Mummy and Daddy love each other, and that they are safe. I imagined sitting together on the couch long after the kids were in bed, comforting one another, encouraging one another, affirming the amazing person we were doing this life with.

And then, as quickly as it had come, the wonder of what could have been, left.

Oh God. Why did You ask me to do this? To rub it in? We're so far from what you brought us here for, God.

No, dear. I brought you both here, fought for you to be here—and you both fought hard with me. You were created for this. You're shining here in Turkey. But you could shine brighter as a couple. This is your time to unite in love as never before. I brought you here to heal your marriage. To bind old wounds. To grant you fresh pride in one another. Both of you have achieved more and coped with more than is normal.

No. I'm not rubbing it in. I didn't ask you to write that list because I thought it would inspire you. I know you feel too far gone for that. Anya, I asked you to make that list because I need you to get angry. Look at what you have been robbed of. Look at what glory I could have had through you and Jeff. This could have been life in its fullness for you! Our enemy gloats. His masterstroke—the easy target—was your marriage.

I warned you both. You've seen other couples here up close. Some have stopped pursuing the dreams they came with. Others have invested time in you, Anya, reached out to you, but now they're struggling just to keep their heads above water. There's isolation and loneliness and physical sickness in so many of my people, especially those who do not know how to resist the devil. But you are all precious to me. I don't want any of you to come strong and leave weak.

Nor do I want you and Jeff to simply settle for a workable solution but two very separate, weak lives. Anya, the enemy has stolen so much already. If you and Jeff don't get angry about this, you could find that Turkey carried a cost I never intended for you. Coming here is not supposed to cost you your marriage, your children, your health or your effectiveness.

The thing is, I died so you wouldn't pay that kind of cost. The sacrifice for you was meant to be a joyful sacrifice, giving up some comforts, some supports, to follow me.

But I died for your provision. You don't need to be homeless. I died for your health. You don't need to be sick. I died for your marriage. You don't have to be alone in this world. Eden is being restored. This life should shout the Gospel of love, of barriers broken, of lavish affection. You've believed lies. You've not resisted. And without the great force I gave you in each other—you stand vulnerable to losing it all.

Satan is ruthless, Anya. He won't stop till there's total destruction. He won't stop with celiac disease. He won't stop with taking just your house. He won't stop with simply confusing and hurting your children. He won't even stop with reducing your influence in this city to nothing. He is the Destroyer. He's the Accuser. There's a whole lot worse up ahead if you both refuse to heed my warning and repent, and come to me that you might be healed.

Lord, how do we come to You? We haven't prayed together, worshipped together, sought You together. My goodness, we haven't slept together, talked together, laughed together, walked together, for a very long time. How do we ever come now to fight together?

Anya, you are right. There are so many aspects of your relationship, that you'll have to address as a couple. Shared wounds. Shared covenants. It shows how incredibly strong your unity is in my estimation.

But I want to show you some special strongholds that are all yours. They've impacted Jeff badly, but they are not his problem. Will you listen?

Of course, Lord. So Jeff was right. I need to sort myself out. It's easier to hear it from You—You who have loved me so tenderly right at my weakest. Thank you, Lord. And sorry for arguing this point with Jeff. I just felt so . . . judged. So put down. It was my pride. I'm sorry. So what are these strongholds?

Are you ready? I'm going to make this very clear!

I'm ready. But Lord, cover me while You draw near. Shelter me from the darkness. Hide me from the taunts of the Accuser. Let Your blood speak *for* me, even as You speak *to* me. I feel so vulnerable. Please don't expose me to the eyes of others. Don't let those demons whisper and point and plot against me now. I'm so very scared.

Anya, I will never make you look foolish. I'm not trying to prove anything to the spirit-realm or to other people.

Anya, look out the window. The sun is rising. A new day is dawning. And I am rising too. Rising with healing in my wings. But for now, those wings cover you. No one can see. It's just you and me. And my blood? It covers you too. No attack can interfere with what we are about to do.

Thank you, Lord. Let me pray that prayer once more . . .

I prayed the Daily Prayer once again, made a cup of tea and put some worship music on. I had learned that in an atmosphere of worship, Satan tends to lose his grip. Not only that, but worship attracts the presence of God like nothing else I know. I began quietly thumbing through my Bible, waiting to see where the Lord would lead me next. What the Lord and I were about to do would require an unhurried stretch of time, and, from my side, a submissive and alert spirit. It was time to step into territory I had never been before.

Later that morning . . .

Oh Lord. I can't believe You've led me here—to Zephaniah chapter three. To the Daughter of Zion.

Before coming to Turkey, I had been asked to speak at a women's conference hosted by our church in Australia. The preparation for my three sessions was a rich time for me, as I asked God to show me what was on His heart for those women at that time.

It began when a little phrase in the middle of the book of Lamentations jumped out at me. *'Daughter of Zion.'* It intrigued me. Amid all the wars and battles and the predominantly male context of the Old Testament, why this reference to a woman? Why a Daughter? And what was the significance of her city?

Over the next three months, I searched and prayed and traced the theme throughout the Bible. As I wrote my talks, I was blown away. This woman's story was my story. It was humanity's story—a story of lost dignity, of shame, isolation, woundedness and bondage— themes common to us all. My heart swelled as I honed in on Jesus, saw how he experienced every aspect of our brokenness, and grasped how, in his death, he bore it all away.

But the story took a surprising turn. Restoration for the Daughter of Zion didn't end with her being whole. It took her to a whole other place—a realm outside the parameters of this world, the spiritual realm, the heavenlies. The Story of the Daughter of Zion, as I called it, was a vibrant and powerful invitation to life on the other side of the torn curtain . . .

I can't believe there's another side to this. Those talks were absolutely anointed, Lord. I love what You gave me. And I thought when I prepared that study, that I was speaking from experience. Now I realize it was also prophetic. A prophetic word for me. Father, thank you. I take these verses afresh for my life today.

SING, O DAUGHTER OF ZION!
BE GLAD AND REJOICE WITH ALL YOUR HEART . . .
THE LORD HAS TAKEN AWAY YOUR JUDGMENTS,
HE HAS CAST OUT YOUR ENEMY.
THE LORD IS IN YOUR MIDST;
YOU SHALL SEE DISASTER NO MORE.   ZEPHANIAH 3:14-15

Thank you, Lord. Rise up for me now. I lay hold of the promise. Cast out my enemy. Let me see disaster no more.

Now for that prayer. *'My dear Lord Jesus . . .'*

Oh God. I can't even go on. How dear You are to me. . .

And then, it was as if the gates of my heart burst, and I was un-done with love for Jesus. I had always believed that Jesus loved me. But I had never *felt* his love. I had always said I loved him too, yet I had never felt that love well up and overflow. I found myself crying from deep within, unstoppable tears that healed and flowed and reassured me all at once. Something shifted in my soul as His love washed over me. *Jesus loved me.* And now I knew it wasn't just words. *I loved him too.*

Anya. Let your tears fall. You're so deeply emotional. You're so deeply spiritual. This is the real you.

Well, I'm hormonal too. A shambles of hormones in messed up proportions.

Yes. When you think of being hormonal, you think of unhealthy responses. You over-react to little provocations. You worry more. You lash out, I know. But I see it a bit differently. I made you to have these cycles. Won't you see it as a gift? You feel pain, discomfort, irritableness. Others give you a wide berth. But daughter . . .

. . . At this time, every month, you are more tender than ever. You feel deeply and express yourself without your usual restraint. And here you are, directing your love to me! It's beautiful! It's what I intended all along. For some people, a holy day or a calendar prompts them to come to me. But in you—in all my daughters—is a natural abandon, the call from within to love, to worship, to be embraced.

Right now, in these few days, you are more able to receive my affection. You crave it more, and you resist me less. You know that when I caress you, when I embrace you, there are no strings attached. No expectations but that you will rest in my love. You are weaker than ever, but you desire for me is strong. This is the time when I can bless you and serve and love you, and you can be sure I am not wanting to use you.

Now, please don't cry anymore. We have prayers to pray and strongholds to break.

Okay. Back to the prayer. '*My dear Lord Jesus . . . I confess here and now that it is all about you, God, and not about me. You are the hero of this story . . .*'

Oh Lord. I so want to be like those people who can say, 'I love the Lord because He healed me when I was most broken.' That's why I am so scared of putting in any effort. I want *You* to be my Healer. I want *You* to be my hero. I'm tired of my useless self. Please God?

'*. . . Forgive me for my every sin. Search me and know me, and reveal to me any aspect of my life that is not pleasing to you . . .*'

    Deceit

Deceit? Is this a stronghold in me? Really?

    Yes

It's not on my list of obvious issues. And my list is long. Please don't confuse me. Is this You speaking to my spirit?

I needn't have worried. Every morning, along with reading the Daily Prayer, I had firmly forbidden the Enemy to interfere. '*In Jesus name, I close my ears and heart and mind to any voice that is not the Lord's. I shut out every distracting voice, every voice of the enemy, even my own carnal reasoning, and I declare I will listen to the voice of God alone.*' Still, it didn't hurt to clarify. The last thing I expected to hear God say was that I needed to deal with Deceit.

    Anya, I said I would make it clear for you. You asked me to reveal any aspect of your life that does not please Me.

    Deceit.

Lord, will you give me something to work with? A memory?
An example?

When you were a young girl, you stood on a little box in your bedroom. Do you remember? You stood tall, looking into the mirror, holding a pretend microphone in your hand, and with all your heart you sang, 'Jesus loves me.' It was beautiful. I delighted in you.

I remembered, all right. Another seemingly petty scenario that had stayed with me over the years. My mum had knocked gently and walked in just as I was about to break into the chorus. I scrambled down, off my box. And though no explanation was required, I found one anyway. I lied. I stammered something to my mum about how my Sunday School teacher had asked me to practice that song, and quickly found something else to do. . .

Anya, that was deceit speaking. Instead of letting your mum see you loving me and baring your soul, you hid. You said your Sunday School teacher had given you the task of singing. You made it about duty, not delight. You knew you were beautiful, but you veiled your beauty. Like Eve who realized she was exposed, you ducked and hid. She hid behind bushes. You hid behind deception.

See? You can deceive others by trying to impress them. By wanting to look more capable or smart or confident or whole than you are. Or you can deceive people by deliberately hiding your strengths, your personality, your loveliness, in the name of humility. One is no better than the other. It's all phony. Like the copy of Windows on your laptop.

Why did I feel the need to deceive? To lie?

You were self-conscience. You thought it was wrong to shine. You were unhealthily self-conscious. Your words of devotion, in song, turned quickly to a lie, a spoken lie. You gave the devil a foothold, and he quickly took advantage of you. Demons don't give that up easily, Anya. For thirty years, they've been shoring up their grip.

One of the hallmarks of a spiritual stronghold is that it gains strength over time. Now, I realized the effect this was having on me, even as an adult. What started as a propensity to lie, had progressed to the point where I didn't even know the real me.

This issue has deepened over the years, hasn't it? It's not getting better. Now I can't express even my love even for Jeff. Not physically. Not with words. I don't seem to be able to express my thoughts properly any more. My spirit has been hidden behind duty for so long I don't even know who I am.

Lord, my son Joseph asked me yesterday what my favorite color is. Lord, I didn't know what to answer. I don't *know* what I really like. I don't have favorite *anythings*. It's as if even expressing a preference would define *me*, and the real *me* has got lost somehow. Oh God . . . what do I *do*?

Name the stronghold, Anya. The Enemy loves darkness, but I've uncovered it for you. You know its name. Bring it into the light. Then we'll weaken it with my Word.

I still felt self-conscious making these sort of declarations out loud; I had to get beyond my simplistic idea of prayer. This wasn't just communing with God, who knows all my thoughts. This was spiritual warfare—and if using our hands is how we get things done in the physical realm, using our words is how we get things done in the spiritual. If I was to demolish a spiritual stronghold, I would need to learn to *say the words out loud*.

In Jesus' name I identify the stronghold of Deceit in my life. I expose the lie I spoke as a child. I call it all into the light.

Now what, Lord?

> *Apply forgiveness, Anya. In so doing, you remove any legal right for Deceit to operate in your life.*

Lord, I bring You all the nakedness I felt when I was seen worshipping. My soul was bare in that moment, and I couldn't handle it. You know how that feels, Lord. You were exposed too. Please forgive me, Lord, that I hid my soul that day and took Deceit as my covering. I wash in your forgiveness. I take a great measure of forgiveness for my lies and deception over all these years. I bathe in your precious blood, Jesus.

And, before all spiritual beings in the heavenlies, I forgive all those who contributed to the insecurity and sense of embarrassment I felt even as a young girl. I release each of them into your forgiveness, Lord. Forgive me, too, for all the hurt I have caused those I love by not being real and upfront. I soak in forgiveness now . . .

Suddenly I felt a whole lot freer. In my mind's eye, I was standing before the Lord, known and seen and heard, and slowly, in His presence I removed the robe of deceit I had woven and worn for too many years. It was then that I realized the impact this stronghold had had on my worship.

Lord, I've not been able to worship You openly ever since that day. I realize now I've always bowed my head in Your presence. I don't know what it's like to lift my face and hold my head and hands high in worship. I feel so bound, Lord, so incredibly self-conscience, even now.

> *Yes, you need to demolish this stronghold. We will do that with my Word, Anya. You've always loved my Word. Now you get to use it! This stronghold came against your voice. Now it's time to open your mouth again and SPEAK!*

I come to break down this stronghold with the word of God. I gaze upon the Lord Jesus and declare that 'in Him was no sin, *nor was any deceit in His mouth.*' (Isaiah 53:9) and that He is my righteousness.

I also declare Eve's story, that resonates so closely with my own. As she openly ate a piece of fruit, God walked in on her, in a sense. He saw her, and like me, when she knew she was exposed, she quickly explained the situation away with the words, '*The serpent deceived me.*'

Satan, the Word of God calls *you* the Deceiver. I

expose you as the one who led me to Deceive. You set me up, but now Jesus will set me free. Jesus is the Way, the *Truth* and the Life. All His words are *true* and I am *in Him*. I declare that I will know the truth in every situation, and the *truth* will set me free!

I had no framework for what I was doing, but by now I was getting in the groove. I sensed that this wasn't something I could really get wrong. I just needed to let loose and hurl truth at this stronghold. For my first go at this, the whole thing seemed to come very easily. It was as if the Lord was as eager to get rid of it as I was. I figured that an ungodly stronghold must have evil operating out of it, and so I went for it . . .

In Jesus name, I cast the spirit of Deceit from me. You must present yourselves before the Lord. You are not to come near me again. You are not to influence or touch my precious husband or my wonderful children. You have no place in my family any longer. In Jesus' powerful name, I cast you out.

I reject Deception for my life. I renounce your claim to me and I command you, and all those demons who work with you, under you or for you, to release their hold on me. In Jesus name, I deny you the foothold you have had. I destroy your stronghold. You have no place in my life. I will not be deceived, or deceive any longer. I will not hide my true spirit, created in the lovely image of God. I will not be rendered unresponsive anymore. Jesus died to set

my spirit free, and call my spirit out of hiding. I declare my voice—free. My body—free. My soul—free. My emotions—free. My worship—free. I declare your stronghold in my life is destroyed.

I'm still right here with you, Anya. It's okay. Let's finish what we began.

Oh Father. What will You do with the rubble of a broken-down stronghold? The barrenness that's left? It's like a tender wound that's been cleaned out but it's still open.

I'll take the rubble and raise up a temple of praise. I'll turn the barren places into springs of water, gushing with beauty and life. My life-giving spirit will awaken you. And the wound? Let me pour the oil of joy upon it. I'll bind up your wounds so they no longer fester. But the healing balm? We will find that together.

Lord, let me now place truth where deceit has been. I call on You Lord, to bless me with integrity. With truth. I want to fully and freely express my love for You.

One by one, verses passed through my soul. The Lord was speaking Psalm 32 over me for my release and my healing:

Anya, in your spirit 'there is no deceit.' You 'acknowledged your sin to me and did not hide your iniquity.' Now, 'I am your hiding place.' Sing again, Anya. 'Rejoice, you righteous, and shout for joy all you upright in heart! Rejoice in the Lord.'

Lord, Amen. 'Praise from the upright is beautiful.'

You've longed to have beauty, Anya. To create beauty. To live surrounded by beauty. To unveil your own beauty. If that's true, then praise. Praise me, just as you once did, as a little girl. Delight in me. Delight in your voice, your poise.

A chorus came to mind, and once again, it was just me in a room, not looking into a mirror but into Jesus' face, and I quietly sang:

Praise the Lord, O my Soul, Praise the Lord.
Praise the Lord, O my Soul, Praise the Lord.
The Lord is good to all, He has compassion on all that he has made.
As far as the East is from the West,
that's how far He has removed our transgressions . . .

And then I gave a shy laugh. I had sung in perfect tune! Had anyone heard, I wondered?!

Day 9

Lord that was a nice little word You sent me this morning. I never bother opening emails from that site. But you prompted and I responded. Now I see why. You still have hope for Jeff and I, don't You?

This was the daily devotion I read, and it reminded me that although I felt desperate about our marriage, our struggles were, in many ways, normal. When everything about our environment, our calling, even our relationship, seemed so magnified, it was a word that brought perspective.

It's Never Too Late

'HOW GOOD AND PLEASANT IT IS WHEN GOD'S PEOPLE LIVE TOGETHER IN UNITY! FOR THERE THE LORD BESTOWS HIS BLESSING, EVEN LIFE FOREVERMORE. PSALM 133:1 NIV

Life has challenges- none more so than in the area of relationships. Parents, children, colleagues, and friends—we all interact in countless relationships every day. Sometimes these relationships can go wrong—disagreements, misunderstandings, circumstances, other people's actions-countless things can go wrong. The enemy loves problems in relationships, so he can divide and destroy. In doing so he's able to cause deep pain in the people directly involved and often many others close to them. Every broken relationship is a win for the kingdom of darkness.

It's a key area for us Christians. We need to be on guard because we need to protect our relationships. They're precious. We must keep them pure and abounding in love. We must have a readiness to humble ourselves for the sake of the relationship. With regard to past relationships I believe the heart and message of the Lord is 'it's never too late.' It never too late to repair or restore a relationship. Maybe we have un-dealt with issues in our relationships. But whether the relationship is ongoing, or broken and abandoned, it's never too late. The Lord can lead and guide our heart to where we need to bring unity in the relationships in our life and, as the scriptural promise says, our actions will command blessing.

I used the prayer at the end as I went into the day . . .

'Father God, thank you for the relationships You've given me in my life and for all the joy they've brought me. I want to be right before You about any broken relationships in my life. Please show me anywhere where I am causing disunity by action, or inaction, and give me the love and the courage I need to make good on these relationships. Lead me and guide me I pray, in Jesus' name, Amen.'

Day 10

I had asked the Lord if I needed someone to help me find the healing I needed, someone to guide our marriage from what felt like disaster to a place of peace again. But being in a country like Turkey, there were very few people I could easily turn to, and I felt vulnerable enough without bringing our relationship issues up. And then, I came across a short personal essay by a woman who had been in Christian ministry most of her life, which stopped me in my tracks and ministered to me all at once. Though I was not an introvert, by any means, yet all my life I had been introspective, and my propensity to entertain streams of unfiltered thought through my head was beginning to do me in.

Father, this daughter of Yours was broken and sitting in a councilors office at age sixty? Oh Lord, my life feels over. I've been wondering if You can really change me, even at thirty-seven? I hear her words, and I agree. . .

'Good things can happen in solitude . . . But there's a dark side to solitude when I crave it above all. The 'I' comes to mean, not only 'introvert', but literally 'I.'

'I don't want you around because I am the one who makes me happy
. . .'

Well Lord, I feel alone, for sure. I love being alone, when I'm healthy. But there's only one person I really long for right now, and that's Jeff. Sure, if he and I together can't get our marriage sorted, there are friends I could call on. But God, I still just wish he and I could try.

Anyway, Lord, You've heard me as I've hinted at my brokenness to others. One girlfriend reminds me of a sermon I should listen to, another gives me a list of ways to be a better wife. But the one that really hurt was the woman who belittled me when I said I needed healing and brushed me off with a recommendation to get professional help for my 'mental health problems.'

I had a tall order. I wanted someone who would be undaunted by my brokenness, approach my issues spiritually, walk me though the journey of healing, and stay around long enough to see me into breakthrough.

In the end, the Lord seemed to articulate the hesitancy on my heart even before I did.

> *Anya, you could ask those women for advice—but that would require so much vulnerability of you, and I don't think you have any more healthy vulnerability left.*

I decided to contact two women we had been friends with in Australia. One was based in Eastern Europe, where she and her husband were in ministry. The other led an online prayer group I was part of. I decided to make contact again and ask them if they would be willing to pray for me as I tried to listen and respond to God. Before I went ahead though, I needed to double-check with the Lord.

Lord, I do want to be sure that our breakthrough comes Your way. I don't want to default to human wisdom when You alone know my heart. Shall I speak to those two women?

Yes—just those two. And just to ask for prayer cover for you . . .
And Anya, don't look to Jeff to answer your questions either. First you need
to know your worth to me, and my love for you. Jeff has burdens too . . .

Day 11

Lord Jesus, I tried to remember a woman in the bible who was hopeless, sick and unloved. I need an example.

> *The only example that will minister to you, Anya, is the Daughter of Zion. You don't need to search or study. I prepared her story for this time. Just read your notes. I prompted you to bring them to Turkey, because I knew they were for now. Read them and ask me to show you the keys. She will be your feminine example.*

Let me start with that prayer for freedom once again. I nearly have it memorized! Thank you for not growing tired of the same words over and over. My dear Lord Jesus. I come to You now to be restored in You . . .

> *Hold on, Anya. Some deliverances are hard won and some are not. I've sent help. Check your inbox.*

Already?

> *Already.*

Oh God. Such grace.

The night before, I had written a quick email to my friend in Australia, then headed to bed.

Hi there! Just wondering if you would consider praying for me especially right now? Talk about broken, my friend. I'm so broken I wonder if there's any end in sight. But I'm seeking God for help, for healing and for deliverance . . . Just feel in need of someone to journey with me a bit. It's mighty lonely over here. And I'm very vulnerable. But please only take me on if God whispers His 'yes' into your spirit. I know your love is poured into many people and places, and I understand if this is one request too many . . .

It was only a matter of hours later—dawn was still a long way off—and already there was a reply!

Oh Anya, my precious sister—tears here. I love you and yes, I will journey with you. I've been trying to find time to share some of my brokenness with you and ask you to journey with me. And you know what, he's already whispered in my ear, and ever since, I've been praying. And no, praying with you is never one request too many—it's an honor . . .

For a moment, my heart welled up with gratitude and love for God's amazing family all over the world. Feeling a whole lot less alone and a whole lot stronger, I found my resolve returning. It was time to make progress.

Now, Anya. Read the story of the Daughter of Zion. Read slowly. Read softly. Let me impress into you what I choose . . .

Dear Lord. I didn't get far along, did I, before you revealed my need.

> *The first thing I want you to notice, Anya, is that under loving, strong leadership and authority, people flourished. That is the context I ordained for life in its fullest, its most wonderful. Living free under loving authority.*

Do you mean Jeff?

> *Yes, dear. My desire is for him to lead you, to provide protection, and to fight for you. And also to love you beyond imagination.*

Have I stepped out from under that leadership?

> *Yes. Long ago. Do you think you ever willingly submitted to him?*

I don't know. I've tried to. A lot of times.

> *Yes, but this isn't something one tries to do. You need to ponder this question.*

Okay.

> *Now—my word of hope. See 2 Kings 19:32? The city faces certain destruction but I declared it must not occur. I declare, 'I will defend this city and save it. . .'*

> *I say the same to you. You're wondering if your marriage is doomed. The end looks near to you, I agree. But now hear my words because I mean it.*

> *'I will defend this marriage, and save it.'*

I don't know anyone who would openly defend our marriage, or even vouch for it, Lord. Even Jeff and I seem to have given up fighting for it.

I never asked the Daughter of Zion to fight for her city, Anya. You were right to reject human, feeble attempts to rescue you and Jeff. It will be a lot more glorious when I do it. I'm rising up. I'm fighting for you two.

What a relief. Help me believe you. Is there a chance this could turn out better than it looks?

Anya, listen now. Stash my admonition and promise away in your heart. Affirm my words with your lips and your spirit. Then let's move on . . .

Before all celestial powers, I affirm the word the Lord has spoken over my life. He ordained that I flourish under loving authority, and He promises to defend our marriage and save it. May His words be established. May all that He ordained, come to pass.

Anya, we need to identify a huge thing in your life, and it's rather terrible.

Okay.

See the Jeremiah 6:2 reference?

Yes. 'The Daughter of Zion is cut off.'

Yes. Remember that phrase, 'cut off.' Right now, you are cut off. Jeff has responded to your brokenness and its resultant ugliness and sin, by cutting you off. In the past, he has responded by waiting for you to 'snap out of it.' This time, he's not even waiting for you. He's given up. It's as if he's cut you off.

I feel that, Lord. It's as if he's not even grieving for me. Sort of like he's relieved to have put me behind him. Maybe the children too. He's changed toward them all. I don't feel his patience, his kindness, his grace any more. I've listened these past few days. He's not just distractedly pushing us aside. It feels like he's cut us off. . .

Let's keep this about you, Anya. Right now, we must not allow fear or bitterness to speak. We must cling to grace. I need you to forgive.

I don't know where to start.

Let me jog your memory. Write as I bring things to mind. We'll make a thorough list.

With the Holy Spirit prompting my memories, I made a list that extended over three pages. In one dot point after another, I listed the many times I was cut off in one way or another.

There were times when I was speaking and had been cut off mid-sentence by someone interrupting or answering for me. There were churches we had been part of, investing deeply in friendships and relationships, only to find that once we moved on, very few of those connections continued. I wrote about the feeling, especially in our early years in churches, of never having enough time to enter into worship before it was seemingly cut short to make way for sermons.

I remembered sudden transitions and the sense of finality over many of our goodbyes – selling houses, leaving schools and friends, moving cities, even the way I had to abruptly leave Albania when war broke out; I recalled the feeling of selling our possessions to go overseas, and the familiar experience of being cut off from 'home' and identity and belonging.

All in all, it was a sobering time as I saw a deeply-entrenched pattern emerge. The reality that much of my lifetime had been characterized by being cut off in various ways, sank in, and I began to feel what the prophets might have described as *lament*.

And then there were the times I felt cut off from Jeff, emotionally, physically, spiritually, and—especially poignant—the sense of being cut off from the blessing I longed for over our relationship when we first started out and announced our engagement.

Dear Lord Jesus. What a broken, sad life. What a mess I am. No wonder Jeff has given up on me. I'm not even remotely functioning well. Every single time I had a chance to shine or to be my true self, or even to get comfortable and adjusted, I've been cut off.

Anya, this is the time to promptly move into forgiveness. This has been hard for you. You can't dwell here. I'll show you why very soon. But now, right now, bring every one of these memories to the cross. Apply my blood to these memories. Let me cleanse the wound.

You need to forgive. Forgive Jeff. Forgive your Mum and Dad. Forgive your friends. Forgive yourself. I'll make sure you have an ample supply of forgiveness if you keep coming back to me . . .

Okay Lord.

Lord I forgive the people who cut me off as I was speaking. Over and over again, others have answered in my place. I forgive them for the words they spoke, so unlike what I would have said. I forgive the shame I felt every time it happened. I bring to you the inferiority it implied. And the hurt I've felt as a result.

I bathe in Your forgiveness, Your grace. I release each of those people into Your forgiveness and mine. Over each of those scenes, I pronounce this word: 'Forgiven.'

Anya, you are doing well. I love how you are proclaiming 'forgiven.' Labelling each scenario with finality and closure. You're not even halfway through, though. But pause a minute. I want to tell you this; I was cut off too. cut off from the land of the living. Isaiah 53:8

I know your pain. You can identify with me in my death. Cutting off leads to death. And I, my child, identify with you. You're not cut off from me. I'm walking this road with you.

Thank you, Lord. Thank you. It all feels very sad. Lord, You know all about the emotional cutting off. I bring to You all the times I have felt emotionally disconnected, cut off from those I love. I see Your lonely tears, your nights of anguish, Your immense longing for faithful companions. I remember Gethsemane and the time You cleansed the temple. No one shared Your emotions then—not the doubts, the anger, the torment of spirit. This cutting off, You know very well.

In the end, Anya, I had to say 'Father, forgive them. Forgive them all. They don't even know what they've done.'

I know. Most of it was never intentional. Never borne of meanness. Most of it is broken people, passing on their hurts to me. So Father, forgive them all. Forgive Mum. Forgive Dad. Forgive generations past. Forgive Jeff. Forgive me. Forgive friends and church leaders. I forgive them all too. They had no idea just what they did.

Lord, now I come to this pattern of continual moving, one country to another, one house to another, one school, one community to another throughout my childhood and right into the present.

Yes, Anya. The transience of your life stands out. You've been uprooted so many times. This has led to a lot of the 'cutting off' situations. And you need to understand that this particular issue is generational.

Both you and Jeff came from people who had left behind their jobs, families, countries, cultures, to get a better life. This was not just an adventurous spirit. There was a spirit of discontent. And a spirit of distrust. They never asked me to bring blessing to them back in their home countries. They went elsewhere to find it.

And you have done the same. I took you to Canberra. That transition was from me. But going back? That was, mostly, your discontentment with not owning a house. You saw you could have more for your money in Brisbane and you wanted it. You didn't wait for me to prosper you in Canberra.

Day 11

You'll need to work through this sometime.

The move to Brisbane cut Jeff off from the Public Service. It took you away from wonderful friends and from a settled life in a gentle environment. I could have brought you to Turkey straight from Canberra—minus the hassle. Please don't brush this aside.

Does this hold the key to our house selling?

Yes. That's all I'll say.

For a few months, we had been trying to sell our house back in Australia. It had become a huge burden financially now that we were away—and we were at risk of getting behind in our mortgage payments.

On top of this, the time difference between Australia and Turkey meant that our phone would regularly ring at ridiculously early hours of the morning as the agent tried to communicate updates with us. We wanted to live fully present to our lives in Turkey, but the house back home was taking a disproportionate amount of our attention.

Together we decided to make the most of a booming house market, and list our home for sale. Naturally speaking, it should have sold right away. We had a huge half-acre property in a sought-after area, with a solid home on it, and demand for housing by far outstripped supply.

But we weren't just getting slow interest in the house. We were getting no interest. No one was even turning up at our open homes. It was becoming obvious there was some other dynamic holding back the sale.

Day 12

Lord Jesus. It's late. I'm tired, but I'm excited by where You're taking me.

First though, I repent of the uncertainty (or the certain doom) I have expressed about our marriage. I've said out loud that I don't know how this will end. *My deliverance?* I have no doubt You will continue this incredible work. *But our marriage?*

I renounce my words of doubt and disbelief. I speak in faith, that, despite all appearances, our marriage will be rescued and redeemed by God.

Also, Lord, thank you for that song that just came to my heart. Did You sing it for me, or was it intended for me to sing for You? Never mind. It was very personal. Made me wonder if this whole teetering-on-the-brink-of-ruin will one day become the very story which delivers Jesus' love to others.

God forgave my sin
In Jesus' name
I've been born again
In Jesus' name
And in Jesus' name I come to you
To share his love as he told me to

He said 'Freely, freely
You have received
Freely, freely give
Go in my name
And because you believe
Others will know that I live.

Oh, and Lord, for the first time ever, today, it felt like I was *being* born again. As if I'm in the birthing process, coming into life. I've never been able to bring myself to say with confidence that I am *born again*, because despite confessing my sin and 'getting saved' as a young child, I don't think I have ever felt fully, vibrantly, alive. I still don't. But I feel hope rising within me that a new creation is going to emerge very soon. Thank you, Jesus.

Day 13

Lord, I know we addressed the stronghold of Deceit. But tonight, I said something to Jeff, and he instantly accused me of using every opportunity to turn a knife into him. It struck me that whatever I say, he still presumes the worst of me. I caught a glimpse of how hurt he is. I've been mean for so long that he just expects it now. Sees it in every action. Hears it in every word.

And there's substance to what he feels. I am so used to saying things with double meanings—saying one thing but meaning another. That's deceit. For my deceit, Lord, please forgive me. For using my words to harm and kill, rather than to bless and build up, Lord please forgive me.

I've told you so often that something prevents me from speaking blessing over my family. The problem appears to be getting worse.

> *You're right. You need to be free to speak, to express your soul; and you need to be heard. But we're not up to that yet. Let's move on through the story of the Daughter of Zion. Which words stand out in Lamentations 1?*

Lord, I'm seeing words like; deserted, desolate, like a widow. That's what stands out. I especially see that verse, 'no one is near to comfort me, no one to restore my spirit.' The Daughter of Zion is ALONE.

Yes, Anya. And whose face did I just show you?

My Nana's.

I want you to explore aloneness. Especially aloneness in marriage.

I remembered my Nana sitting on the couch at my uncle's house. I would have only been nine or ten years old, I suppose. The whole family was there, all the children and grandchildren . . . perhaps it was Christmas. But I remembered how sad she looked, as if everyone was partying while she seemed ignored, unnoticed, left out. I could see my uncle sitting beside her and putting his arm across her shoulders, trying to perk her up.

And the blazingly obvious question, which had never entered my mind until now was, 'Where on earth was Grandad?' She looked like a widow. Looked grieved. Lost in her inconsolable darkness. But he was alive. He would have been there.

Had he told her how lovely she looked in the blue dress? How her eyes shone at the thought of her family? What a wonderful mother she had been to those three boys? How it still made him proud to be her husband? Did he comfort her as she realized the Christmas gathering was no longer at her home? Did he sit with her to laugh and enjoy the moment the children opened presents?

I suspect he was emotionally, spiritually and physically *gone* and she was alone. She with the poetry. She with the family history research, her books, her love of fine china and rose bushes and porridge served with cream and demerara sugar. When did her feminine spirit die? When did her heart break into its last fragment? Long before she said her final farewell to the man who once won her heart, I suspect. Long before dementia stole her mind and her every remaining happy memory.

Oh Lord. My lovely Nana. She was like a widow, even in marriage. My mum used to say to me, 'You're just like Nana. You're Nana all over again,' and I guess now she was right.

> *You feel alone in your marriage, as if Jeff's deserted you—left you desolate—despite the shared roof.*

Yes, I not only deeply understand my Nana, I *feel* it with her. I am living her story. Oh God! Save me from such a wasted life. Such destruction of beautiful potential. Save my *daughters*, Lord.

> *This is a spirit, Anya, passed across the generations. Now it's in you. You, even now, can discern that there is a spirit of Desolation in you and in your marriage. Think of all the times you've felt desperately alone.*

Okay. I'll make another list. Please let me recall the things that have opened a door for this spirit of Desolation. I don't want to be random here, Lord. Please help me know how this spirit got so heavy within me.

My mind went to my childhood. There were six years between my sister and me. I realized that I had often felt alone, even in a family of six.

I remembered the mornings I would get onto the school bus, only to be greeted by children laughing and teasing me about my name. Mum would wave until the bus was out of sight, and as the bus pulled away, I remember feeling more and more alone.

Years later, I started university. My mind went back to the day mum and I sat on the bed in a tiny barely-furnished room on a college campus. She was crying deep, decades-old tears of loss and regret and grief and I was trying to be brave—to convince her I was happy. But as soon as she left and it was just me and an empty room, the aloneness felt literally painful.

The feeling was similar when, as a wife and mother to two little boys, we moved to a new city. Jeff had been offered a wonderful job, and within weeks, we had relocated. I looked out the window of our temporary inner-city apartment as the rain poured down and the cars lined up at the intersection below; I knew no one in that city, and that day I sat numbly for hours . . . alone.

Then there were the days Jeff was working in another city for half of every week; I would keep the home running, but we all missed him terribly—I'd say goodnight and put down the phone, settle the four little children into their beds and then lock the house, turn off the lights, and wish away the hours, feeling, once again, alone.

Now we were in Turkey. I missed chatting with my dad, missed my brothers and my sister, missed having a cup of tea with mum and watching the cousins play. Jeff seemed lost in his own pain. I related to the Daughter of Zion, who found no one to comfort her. And then, in my mind's eye, I could see the multitudes of women all across the world who felt so terribly alone, and in that moment, it was as if I could identify with them all.

> *You must cast out this spirit of desolation, Anya or you will always feel deserted. Your whole life will be one of tears. Widowhood is not my plan for you. Cast this monster out. You'll need to subdue it and bind it first. You'll need to renounce its claim to you and your family line, especially to your daughters and the women who shall follow.*

> *Desolation and Loneliness work together. In my authority, dismiss them both. Cast them out. Hand them over to me.*

In Jesus' name, I declare that *'it is not good for man to be alone.'* I also declare that the Lord has said, *'I will never leave you.'* Desolation is not my lot in life.

In Jesus' name, I command the spirits of Desolation and Loneliness to release their hold on me. Remove every attachment you have to me—in Jesus' name I render you weak and powerless. You may not draw strength from one another or collaborate together, and I forbid you to seek retribution against anyone I love for what I am about to do. In the name of Jesus, I bind you. You are to leave, and present yourself before the Lord, never to return. In Jesus' name, I cast you out.

There is another spirit working with them, and it would be best to deal with it now.

I know its name. Neglect.

Yes, Neglect. Another generational spirit, passed down through the women in your family.

Lord, I think of how my Nana spent her teenage years in Fiji. She seemed to flourish there, but still, she was obviously not being cared for by her own family. She had an amazing love of art. She wrote books and poems, but who was there to nurture her gift? Who was tending to all that was in her? It was the same with my mum. She longed for singing lessons—but instead she got told to be quiet, to stop the incessant singing. It breaks my heart. Neglected souls, neglected talent. You had so much in your heart for our line of women, Lord . . .

Neglected souls trouble me most. You have been neglected too, and you can see it for what it is now. This spirit got in, and it has a deep hold. Neglect does not let go easily. You need to remember that, Anya, so you can muster your determination to cast it out.

I paused for a while, letting the scenarios flow through my mind and heart. There was no sense of blame or accusation towards people. I could see that neglect was something we had all been subjected to, and I felt fresh compassion for those who had carried such a capacity to nurture all that was in me, yet had been too wounded and under-nourished themselves to see it through. I wanted to go back and give them a second chance at life—one without neglect in the mix—just to see what each of us might have been.

One season of my life stood out though, a season of darkness. I didn't know about being broken-hearted back then. I just knew I was in a very dark place in my mind and heart, and it felt as if a thick blanket of despair was closing in around me. Jeff was the only person who drew near to me through that time, and I credit my eventual breakthrough to his loving perseverance and his prayers. Even so, the only words of Scripture that I resonated with at that time were these, spoken by King David. *'No one cares for my soul.'* (Psalm 142:4 NKJV) A sense of neglect had consumed me.

Lord, I even felt like You had neglected me, to be honest.

> *I know. You were bound by neglect. But I have always had people in your life that were entrusted with your care. Neglect of woman, in particular, is a tool of the enemy, and I fight for the opposite. Even in your darkest hours, I had Jeff there to care for you. That's also why I want widows to be especially looked out for. If women don't flourish, the world I love cannot flourish. Nurture is my desire for all women. Then they nurture in response. Start to hate this spirit, Anya.*

Now I could see that this was not a simple attack on my life. This was a scheme of the enemy—a coalition of evil, working together. I needed to get a clear picture of what was going on.

Lord Jesus—how many spirits afflict me? What are we doing here?

> *Draw a picture, Anya. Start with a castle. Like a fortress. Make it big.*

I began to sketch as the Holy Spirit gave me details.

Now draw five figures. Inside the walls. Not men. Draw lots of appendages. No features.

Okay.

Now write their names. I've told you most of them.

I only know three. Desolation, Neglect and Loneliness. Please tell me the names of the other two.

Command them to reveal their identity to you. They need to realize that when you speak, they must respond.

Immediately two unexpected words came to mind.

Their names are Lovelessness and Self-absorption.

Now describe what they have brought to your life. What sort of place do they inhabit?

Toxicity. Mockery. Ingratitude. Bitterness.

I added the words. As my drawing took shape, the Lord took all the confusion out of the spiritual scenario I was dealing with. The more I saw what this spiritual stronghold *looked like*, the more confidence I had to address it. But first, I wanted to talk this through with God.

Lord, can You talk to me about Lovelessness? I know that I don't feel love easily. I *know* my parents love me, and I can say it as a fact, but I don't *feel* their love. I feel people's displeasure, not their delight.

> *I delight in you Anya.*
> *You want a restored marriage. Let's talk about that.*

That's easy. I am numb. I can't receive love. Jeff says *I love you,* and I hear it with my ears, but I don't hear it in my spirit. When he touches me, I feel it physically but my soul can't respond. I've never been able to reciprocate freely. I have no memories of showing him love outside of doing my 'duty' as a wife. I think I love him by cooking for him or ironing a shirt. Or giving him sex. But it's not out of delight in him. It feels like duty. But I do love him, God, don't I? Why can't I feel love? Am *I* loveless?

No, daughter. You're full of love. You've just been very, very bound by this spirit.

You can't image what is in store when you cast it out. Now, let's talk about the last enemy spirit. This one works with all the others and strengthens them.

Its name is Self-absorption.

Yes. And he leaves you mulling, brooding, analyzing, and proud; he kills spontaneity.

He loves to invade your personality. You need to cast him out too.

Please give me the process for this. Do I deal with them individually, or together?

Start with the strongest one first. Desolation.

Name the spirit. Call it forth; rebuke it.

Subdue it with my Word. Renounce its claim on you. And its generational claim.

Then command it to release its hold. Bind the spirit.

Cast it out. And send it to my presence. I will be there, ready to banish.

Okay. Lord, protect me. Protect my family. Let's do this.

In my authority in Christ, I did as the Lord had instructed me. It was short, simple, and it worked. Immediately I felt a weight of heaviness lift off me. Then the Lord gave me a verse—one that touched my heart profoundly.

> YOU SHALL NO LONGER BE CALLED 'FORSAKEN' . . . NOR
> . . . 'DESOLATE.' YOU SHALL BE CALLED 'HEPHZIBAH'
> (DELIGHT), 'BEULAH' (MARRIED). ISAIAH 62:4 NIV.

Dear Father, You are so kind. That spirit of Desolation? What a relief to have it gone. And thank you for that verse!

Then I finished the job. I grouped the other spirits together, along with a little helper called 'Duty'—bound them, rebuked them, and cast them out as one big pack. I declared them all bereft of their claims to me and to all the women after me. It was time to rewrite the history of my family line.

Lord, forbid these spirits to ever return. I, with you, forbid them to harm us or interfere in my marriage or my daughters' or granddaughters'— to a thousand generations.

Draw near to us, Lord. And show me what is next.

Day 14

Daughter, those terrible demons inhabited a stronghold. They made their walls thick and strong. Their fortress remains. It's time to break it down. The stronghold they erected and operated within is called Self-pity.

Before all celestial powers I come, in Jesus' name, to identify the stronghold of self-pity in my life. To weaken its foundations, I declare that, in Christ, I am completely blessed.

I have every spiritual blessing in Christ. I have life—abundant life. I am chosen in him, loved unto death by Him, cherished by Him. He has redeemed my life, renewed my strength, forgiven all my sins, healed my spirit.

I lift my eyes up—*off me*—to the hills. My help is from the Lord. He *rises* to help me.

Now, in His name, I break down the stronghold of Self-pity in my life. I tear it down, stone from stone, until it is reduced to rubble. I raze it to the ground. I declare this stronghold *demolished*. This home of demons is now *destroyed*. There is no place for replacement enemies to set up habitation. Where this stronghold has existed in my life, I declare there is now just a new, wide spacious piece of me—a vast new territory taken back for the Holy Spirit of God to set up residence.

Thank you, God, for that victory.

Day 15

Father, it's hard to believe that this is the same me, same husband, same marriage!

I didn't do anything after breaking down that stronghold, other than cook up a decent breakfast and ask Jeff if he was okay. He looked exhausted.

I asked You, Father, to lead me in our marriage. I determined to do nothing in my own strength or of my own initiative.

All glory to You, God. What a joy to unite with You, follow Your lead, and to find hope and healing and comfort with You in your heavenly realm. I feel as if we have battled in the heavenly places, then watched as the victories there are transferred to earth.

Last night, late, I spoke with a friend, sharing just a little of this journey. I said that I felt like I was being changed and transformed and that God would complete what he had begun. But I also told her how I didn't know how our marriage would end. How on the surface, it wasn't looking good.' Truth is, it looked *over*.

In these past weeks, Lord, I have prayed, slept and woken to deal with the demons. That's all.

It's all for You, Father. All the victory of Your Son at the cross. It's all You—the victorious Trinity, working in beautiful unity, and, so kindly, allowing this broken wretch, in. But I don't feel broken anymore; I feel freed. I know we have more ground to take in my life, but something big has changed. I love You! I desire You! Not just because time with You gives me time away from family, either! Somehow You appear to me as a God of love, my Shepherd, my Father, my Beloved.

Some things really are too sacred to speak of, aren't they, Lord? May I just tell you that when Jeff, without a word, reached out for me, drew me close and held me, I felt like I'd come home. I didn't want to get out of there. My spirit felt at rest. I think I even *felt* his love for me.

It's today, for the first time in my life, that words like *new creation*, *born again*, '*free indeed*' and '*more than conquerors*' don't seem so overrated. For the first time ever, I can relate to the way Your Word sounds! Today, I am a new person. Old things have passed away. This looks a lot like 'newness of life'—like You have made all things new, and that there really is, even for me—for us—a hope and a future. This is the first time ever, Lord, that I've been able to read Romans chapter six, seven and eight, and place myself in there, right the way to the end!

I delight with you, my child. Angels rejoice with you too. We're all very glad about what has transpired. It's a joy to welcome the 'sons of men' among us here in the heavenlies.

Lord, I'm so very tired. I feel as if I've *really* fought a battle.

You have, and it's cost you a lot of sleep and a lot of energy. You're weak but a victory has been won.

Now take care. The enemy is nasty as ever. He is not pleased. So, do as I say, and I will care for you and protect you.

Anya—sleep when you can. I will grant you deep, restorative sleep. Accept the love and kindness of Jeff and the children. I will minister healing and comfort and strength through them, to you.

And pray that prayer for freedom again. It's full of worship, truth, and 'asking rightly'. Hearing you pray those words gives me joy, and allows me to rise up for you. Use them today. One day, when you're stronger, you may not need those words so much. But today, pray them, and worship me.

Day 16

Father, I rested, as you said. Why do I feel so wiped out? I'm still so weak.

Do you feel that way in your spirit?

No! Not that I feel exuberant, but my spirit does seem to be alive and well. Quietly alive and well, I guess.

There have been times when your body has been strong but your spirit bound.

I hate to see your physical weakness, but to me you look healthier than ever.

Yes. Thank you for what you have done in me. Makes me think of that song, '*Let the weak say, I am strong. Let the poor say, I am rich. Let the blind say, I can see. It's what the Lord has done in me.*'

Oh and Lord, thank you for those other beautiful songs you led me to on Sunday. It was so good of Jeff to take all the children to the park so I could rest, and I felt like I totally squandered the time. But when that song came on the radio, I realized I was meant to be home to hear it. Those words are beautiful. Whoever sang it, her voice is beautiful!

Blessed Redeemer, Precious Redeemer
Seems now I see Him on Calvary's Tree
Wounded and bleeding, for sinners pleading
Blind and unheeding, dying for me.

I want to give you more and more music, Anya. In heaven, words are more often sung than spoken. I think you will start to enjoy music again.

Oh God, thank you. I've missed variety in music. Here in Turkey, just accessing music feels so . . . *digital*. Search, download, file, listen, upload . . . Lord I miss my piano. I miss going to concerts. I miss the singing in church.

Bring me your desires. I prefer live music too. *smile* I think music is best accompanied by sunrises and starry nights, mountain streams and snow-capped peaks, beautiful dresses and graceful dance, passionate voices and a captivated audience. Wait on me. Look for me!

Day 17

You give me hope in so many ways, Lord. I was just looking at the little drawings and notes the children gave me when I was feeling so low. When Joseph gave this to me, all in a beautifully labelled envelope, he said, 'Mum, you're smiling in my picture.'

Lord, thank you for the way Joseph just naturally ministers music and beauty and art and drama! He really blessed me with that picture. *You* blessed me through him. You prophesied to me through him!

And Eric's offering—*oh God*. After my meltdown, tears all around the table, five of us sobbing . . . he went to his desk and wrote each of us a note. What a true encourager he is. He gave us the gift of Your word, and slipped each carefully chosen verse in his lovely handwriting under our side plates at the next meal.

Oh God, it was just what each of us needed. Bless that boy. His heart is tender. His strength is in you. He's a rock for our family, right there beside Jeff, bringing strength and solidarity. I *so* needed to know I was loved by you, and he perfectly reminded me of that. Thank you for Eric, Lord.

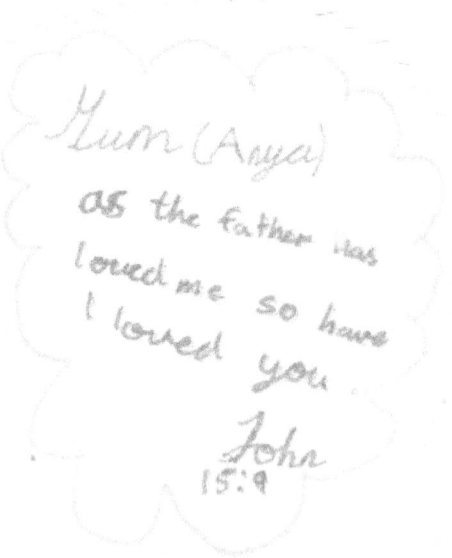

And Evie. Oh, how I love that girl. What a gentle, deep, creative soul. She too, took paper and pencils. She knows the tools to use to speak my love-language. If only there were a category just for me! It would be art-photos-paper-pencils-poetry-words-sayings-melody-nature-beauty-sentimentality! She speaks my language exactly.

And then Liberty. She is so soft towards me. She comes close and sighs. She kisses me and presses her perfect cheek to mine and tells me I'm *so beautiful* and somehow, when it's her speaking, I believe her. She *sees me* as beautiful.

Oh darling child, just-turned-three. She is like music to my soul. So easily affected. So delighted by little things. Is she the child—the dancing, singing, carefree child—that I could have been? She ministers deeply to me, Lord. Even when she is troubled, and her own spirit is all stirred up, she ministers to me. Lord, I love this girl. Set her free day after day. *Liberty*, indeed. She brings me life!

Day 18

Father, I worship You.

And I receive your worship.

I don't know what to do about some things though. Jeff has been so incredibly kind since that whole demon-stronghold morning. We can talk again, which is nice. *smile* But a few times, he has mentioned things and I've responded but I still don't feel like he's really heard my heart. It's like he's listening to my words, Lord, but not hearing my *soul*. I still feel unknown, and, I guess, a bit sidelined.

I know. But you are seeing the consequences of the real problem, and you need to seek me for the way forward. I have more healing to bring to you. Don't focus on these feelings with Jeff. Turn your eyes back to me.

Let me walk you through, a step at a time. Let me reveal what you need. I know how to heal. I know the order it must be done in. I know how the spiritual interfaces with the physical, and I can change anything in the physical realm if you will let my Spirit be united with yours. So, give me your feelings and keep bringing the thoughts and interactions you have with Jeff before Me. Do not judge. Keep this journey between you and me.

PART TWO

God had healed wounds I never realized I had been carrying. Now, it was time to fight for my freedom. I started by casting off chains of distrust and blame in my own life, and before I knew it, I was fighting for the future of an entire city. But the counter-attacks came thick and fast. Even as I got started, it was clear that the enemy was not going to give in without a fight.

Day 19

Okay, Lord. So how do we move forward?

Keep going with the Daughter of Zion story. We only got a few pages in.

Lord, I relate to her chains. These words ring true for me: '*Her bonds are heavy and they make her tired.*' You're my counsellor, Holy Spirit. What are the things that keep me from a light hearted, carefree way of life? What prevents me from dancing and laughing and showing happiness? Lord, what's in me feels *locked in*. I still can't seem to express what I feel inside. Lord, please show me my chains.

Anya, you know how huge the last issue was we dealt with? This one is big too. That's why you needed to rest these past few days.

But now it's time to move forward. Speak to your fear. Speak to your inertia.

Declare that you will boldly confront your chains.

With faith in Christ, I cast fear aside, push tiredness and inertia away. In the name of my loving Savior, He who accepts me, loves me and delivers me, I will now listen, respond and deal with these chains.

Well done. Now, one more thing. You need to boldly declare that Jeff is not the problem. He has never held you back. In fact, he has shown you what freedom looks like.

I now openly declare that Jeff has never held me back from expressing myself. He is not the enemy. My chains are *my chains*, and the bondage in my life is from the real Enemy—it's his works I now come to fight against.

Now, Anya. Chains make you a prisoner. You can squirm all you like, but they won't fall off. When you're chained, you are not really your own anymore. Chains need to be unlocked. There must be a key.

Show me the key, Lord.

The key is this, Anya: At the cross, we were all bound. All three of us. Let me explain.

I, the Father, voluntarily held back, so that my Son could die. I longed to reach out to my Son. I wanted to rescue Him. But out of love for you, I held still. My face was contorted with anguish. But I could not let Him see my face. I could not allow the least expression to show. All I could do was turn away.

And you, Holy Spirit?

I longed to comfort. I wanted to bolster Him—to speak words of truth into Jesus' soul as he suffered. I ached to assure Him that His father still loved Him. I wanted to offer Him promises, to fill Him—to pour my love into Him. If ever I longed to fully express my True self, it was on that day. I too, could show no expression. I too was alone, with inward groanings, unheard, hidden.

Lord Jesus?

Anya, they bound me. My arms were tied to the cross. I couldn't praise. I couldn't run or walk, or even straighten my back. I know about feeling like what others think is important. When I was bound I had to stand, exposed, before Pilate and Herod. They asked me a simple question, 'Are you the Son of God?' and I kept silent.

I couldn't praise.
I couldn't express my love.
I couldn't reassure my friends.

I was bound, and the only expressions I made were crude and simple. No one could see the anguish or the love that was in my heart as I stood on trial. That day, Anya, I took every aspect of your bondage.

There's more though, isn't there?

Yes! You're listening well now. *smile* When I died, I went into a prison. The locks were huge, and the chains—everywhere there were chains and prisoners; tired-looking prisoners—they were thick and heavy. The poor souls were not even struggling any more.

Oh, Anya, it was the first thing I did after I gave my life. I broke into that prison. I took the key. And—greatest joy of my life! I went about unlocking those chains. I set the captives free. Prisoners who had forgotten how to stand up, Anya, let alone dance or clap or sing! Anya, you should have seen it! They were free!

I blessed them all, lifted them up—then led them forth out of that vile place. For the first time ever, all those people were free! Unshackled. Delivered from the enemy. It was my triumph. It still is. I still love to set captives free.

Oh! Loving, Holy Trinity. You're making me cry. You are wonderful, all of You. God—how do I take what You've told me and unlock my own chains?

Dear child. Let us unlock your chains.

Right at that moment, my mind was filled with negative thoughts about Jeff. The more love I felt for God and all he had done, the more I seemed to despise Jeff. Thankfully, the Lord knew my mind, and had something to say about the dark thoughts that kept finding their way in.

Those thoughts are not my thoughts, Anya. The Accuser stands before you, speaking to you, but he's pointing his finger at Jeff. He wants to keep you bound. He wants to stifle all you could do and be if you were truly one as we are one.

What do I do?

Resist the devil, and he will flee from you.

How?

Use my Word. Speak truth.

Okay. To all principalities and powers I say, *God joined us together, and you may not separate us.* The truth is, Jeff loves me. He promised to always love me. I stand with Jeff. I side with him. I am not a captive to your intentions, because Jesus came to set captives free. In turn, I take my godless thoughts captive. Every distracting, divisive thought about Jeff, I now bind in Jesus' name and bring them all to Christ. Thank you, Lord, that You will free me and give me the mind of Christ.

> *Now worship me, dear child. Pray to Me.*

I had fought back with truth, and I followed it up with songs. One by one, as they came to my mind, I sang in order to silence the Enemy and shut out his voice from my mind.

I sang '*May the mind of Christ me Savior live in me from day to day . . .*' I sang about Jesus' death, and about His ultimate triumph. '*Up from the grave He arose. . .*'

Still the unkind thoughts flooded in. My mind had become a battlefield, and I wasn't winning easily.

> *You're still battling in your mind, Anya. You're doubting my words. You have always been told that the only reliable way to hear from me is in my word—my written Word.*

Yes, and when I looked for verses about You freeing captives, it wasn't that clear to me. Am I heading in the wrong direction? I need to know. Satan deceives. He imitates You. I need to know if I really heard Your voice, or if it was a hoax. I need the right key to unlock this mess of chains.

In Jesus name and authority, I forbid lying spirits to speak into my mind. I declare that I am His, and His sheep hear *His* voice, and follow Him. His words give life. I reject all other voices now, and open my ears to hear *His* voice.

Anya, those words this morning? They led you to awe of Me. To worship and wonder, to hope and confidence. Your spirit communed with my spirit. Those words exalted me, exalted the Trinity, exalted Christ and His finished work.

That's not how Satan speaks. His words cause you to doubt me and question my good heart. His words are designed to confuse you and to belittle Me. But you heard my words, Anya. Not one Word of Scripture disagrees with what I said. But if you are to mature, you must get used to listening and putting your hope in all my words. I spoke long ago through the fathers and the prophets, I spoke through Jesus my Son, and I also speak with you by my Spirit. You are learning to trust my voice.

In You, Lord, I put my trust. Do not let my enemy gloat. Do not allow him to triumph over me. *Please*—how do I get free from these chains?

Anya, this will be hard for you. But I'm asking you to just come into my presence.

Linger with me. Gaze into my face. Behold my wounds. Sense my Spirit. Come into my Sanctuary. For now, lay aside the notebook and pen. It's time for us to commune face-to-face.

This was my Garden of Gethsemane moment. Jesus had asked me to be with Him, to keep Him company, and all I felt was an overwhelming need to rest. I didn't see the change of tactic. All I felt was exhaustion, and in giving in, I realized later I had missed a sacred opportunity.

Father, I tried. Really. But I fell asleep. I'm *so* tired, Lord. Sorry.

Anya, we're losing ground. This is not complex.
Your ability to express yourself has been bound on earth. In heaven, it's not like that. You need to loosen these chains on earth and it will be done in heaven. In the spiritual realm, you will be free and that will become your reality on earth too.

In the name and authority of the Lord Jesus I declare that Jesus came to set captives free. I declare that it is for *freedom* that Christ has set me free. His cross avails for me. He has broken every chain. He opens prisons and He leads His people forth. In Him, I pronounce my chains are broken.

I break off the fear of looking hypocritical.
I break off the chain of concern for outward appearance.

I break off the chain of paranoia about false emotion.

I break off the chains of my past that say that women should be silent and that children should be seen and not heard.

Many occasions when my self-expression was stifled came to mind, and again, I brought forgiveness to each memory. I realized that over the years, I had become less and less expressive, less inclined to let others see the real me.

Lord, I ask forgiveness for participating in the bondage, for holding onto my chains. I'm sorry for setting aside my creativity and my writing. I'm sorry for not bringing all of who I am to our marriage and for holding back when I should have affirmed Jeff's ideas and thoughts. I also come for forgiveness for stifling my children along the way—for trying to shape their expressions when they were just being true to themselves.

I see that Satan has kept me from profound and exuberant expression and replaced it with outbursts that are . . . ugly. He has bound my ability to show delight, praise, joy, hope, worship, thankfulness, and left me conveying disdain, complaints, sadness, despair, blasphemy, ingratitude.

Now, in Christ, I cast aside the chains He broke for me. I lay them aside. I proclaim to all celestial powers that I am not bound. I am loved and indwelt by the Spirit of the Lord, and where the Spirit is, there is freedom.

Jesus says to me,

'AWAKE, AWAKE. CLOTHE YOURSELF WITH STRENGTH. PUT ON
THE GARMENTS OF SPLENDOR. SHAKE OFF YOUR DUST. RISE UP.
SIT ENTHRONED. FREE YOURSELF FROM THE CHAINS ON YOUR
NECK, O CAPTIVE DAUGHTER OF ZION.' ISAIAH 52:1,2 NIV

*Anya, you have written from your heart and your words are powerful. But
for them to take effect, you must speak them aloud.*

I was thankful for the reminder. It was as if the Lord was coaching
me until speaking out truth and freedom came naturally and easily.

Day 20

I did it, Lord! But other than my arms feeling literally sapped of strength, I can't tell any difference. I've worked on demons and strongholds, but this sort of binding and loosing is such a new thing for me.

Anya, what you just released on earth, I now release in heaven. Before me, you are free. Let the gaze and thoughts of others grow small. Sing for me alone. Dance before me. Worship just for me. Even love Jeff, knowing my smile is on you both.

Day 21

God, I feel like such a hopeless wife. Jeff keeps trying to bless me, and I keep throwing it back in his face. I can't seem to see good in him until after I've criticized and demeaned him. God, does this ever end? I hate myself—even more so for thinking we were making headway and then realizing I'm as hopeless a case as ever.

Tonight, Jeff asked if I wanted to watch a movie with him, Lord, and when I hinted that we could talk through this stuff instead, he just switched off and eventually went to bed. It's like he just couldn't be bothered. Mind you, I know how he feels. We're so tired of going around and around the same issues. Deep down we both just want to be free to enjoy life together.

Sorry for getting sidetracked, Lord. You must have more rewarding people to work with.

Day 22

Anya, you are still my daughter. Despair and discouragement don't become you. You have hit a glitch, and yes, you have started to lean on your own understanding rather than to keep listening. Go back to your prayer for freedom. As you pray, listen.

LET MY PRAYERS BE SET BEFORE YOU LIKE INCENSE.   PSALM 141:2 NIV

'My dear Lord Jesus. I come to you now to be restored in you . . .'

I know what You're saying, Lord. My pride must be the next victim in this battle for freedom. Amazing how I can feel so pathetic and yet be so full of pride.

Yes. But pride only bows at the cross. It's a put-it-to-death scenario. It needs to be crucified. Pride belongs to your old nature, not the new creation I want for you. You can see how pride comes before destruction—you have come close to being destroyed. You see, pride will kill you if you don't kill it. We're not dealing with the devil here, Anya. This is the flesh. It's the world. 'The pride of life is not of the Father, but is of the world.' 1 John 2:16

Lord, remove my old nature. I circumcise my heart unto

God. I take my place in Your cross and death. I have died with You to sin, and to my flesh, to the world and to the evil one. I crucify my pride with all its sinful desires.

Anya, you prayed that paragraph of your freedom prayer. You brought pride to the place of crucifixion. Now, let's replace pride with humility.

Many years earlier, I had memorized the second chapter of Philippians—a chapter about the humility of Jesus. Now I personalized the chapter and turned it into prayer. This is how it sounded . . .

Lord Jesus, I long for consolation in Christ, for comfort in Your love and Jeff's, for fellowship in the Spirit, for affection and mercy. I want to be like-minded with Jeff, having the same love, being of one accord, of one mind. I confess that I have lived so long through selfishness and conceit, but now, I take lowliness of mind, and with Your help, I esteem Jeff as better than myself. I choose to look out, not only for my own interests, but for his, and for others' too.

Father, let this mind be in *me*, which is also in Christ Jesus. I do not cling to equality with You or with Jeff. I set aside my reputation and I ask for the heart of a servant—one who loves her husband, and does not desire any other. Just as Jesus, your Son, became one of us, I too declare and recognize that I am only human. I share common humanity, common frailty, common sin, common foolishness and brokenness. I humble myself, submit myself to you and to my husband, and take my place in death to self and sin and pride.

I heard your prayer. It has been placed before me as incense.

Day 23

Dear Lord Jesus. I'm so tired. Is there more breakthrough in sight? I love, love, love these early morning hours, but during the day I can't find any energy and in the evening, the tiredness hits me and I fall asleep. Is it nearly time to look up and see Your salvation?

> *Today is very significant, Anya. But you have some more spiritual work to do.*

> *We need to break down the disrespect you show to Jeff.*

Oh, good. I hate it! I can't remember ever showing true respect to him. I feel it though. You know that if there's one guy I respect, it's Jeff.

> *Yes, but you don't show it. You communicate disrespect.*

Lord, can You show me what respect looks like and sounds like?

Okay, let's do a little Bible Study. I'll show you where to look. You open your eyes and ears. First, read about Gamaliel.

Acts 5:32-40 Gamaliel was respected by all the people. The thing that stands out, Lord, is that when he spoke, they took his words to heart, they listened properly, heard what he was saying, and '*they agreed with him.*'

Lord, when Jeff speaks, I often criticize or shrug him off or outright contradict him. I default to playing devil's advocate, like it's a favorite game. How nasty, now I think about it. Jeff always speaks well of everyone. He's full of wisdom. How do I change my communication?

> *You need to slow down. Listen, Anya. You'll find out how powerful that can be! Anya, many couples disagree on things, and it leads to conflict. You, however, agree with Jeff on nearly everything, only you rarely let that show. You mask your true self and rob your marriage of oneness. Do you see?*

Yes.

> *Now read Hebrews 12:9.*

Hebrews 12:9 'Furthermore, we have had human fathers who corrected us, and we paid them respect. . .'

I'm struck with the concept of respect being something we *pay*. Like it's the right and honest thing to give in return for someone's investment in our lives.

> *Yes. If Jeff serves you, loves you, honors you, praises you, provides for you,*

watches over you, yearns for you . . . respect is what you return. Respect is to receive his investment in you and to allow all he is and does to bless you. Right now, you resist his blessing by not affirming him.

Sorry, Lord.

Now, let me gently lead you back to Ephesians 5:33.

Ephesians 5:33 'Let each one of you . . . love his own wife as himself, and let the wife see that she respects her husband.'

Hear my entreaty, Anya. See that your respect your husband.

Father, I want You to take my disrespect and transform it. I want *You* to free me to express respect and to give Jeff the grace to receive it.

Yes, this too must be a deep work.
I'm glad you are not trying to reform, or to obey in your own strength.

How do we proceed?

Let's walk through your life.

Well, I don't remember a lot of respect from the women to the men. My family were very critical.

Go back to your grandparents. Where is the problem?

Mostly in my Nanna. She demeaned and belittled my Grandad all the time. Quietly, but always cutting and malicious. Even words that on the surface could sound kind or sweet, had an underlying blade to them. I'd say perhaps she hated him. That sounds harsh, but it's how it came across.

> *Realize, Anya, that respect and love go together. You can't say you love Jeff if you do not show him respect. Now, renounce your Nanna's disrespectful words and actions. Annul that part of her legacy. Acknowledge that she too was manipulated by the devil. She never knew Me. Forgive this legacy and release her into my forgiveness.*

Father, I bring this awful legacy of disrespect for husbands to You. I cut it off in Jesus' name for me and for the generations of women that shall follow me. I release my Nanna, even at the end of her life, into Your grace and care. I ask that You meet her and cleanse her and wash her sins away . . . You have a very kind heart, Lord, full of compassion and tender mercy.

> *Anya, I want to come now to the next generation—your mum's generation. Those women truly loved and respected their men. That's why they married them. But they were not raised with the language of respect either . . .*

> *But there's more to the story. I feel sorrow over this situation. The Enemy doesn't want women to express what's in their hearts, and most men don't know how to fight for their wives. Think about how your mum loved to sing. Apologize for all the times you felt embarrassed by her singing. Remember how she loved to rearrange the house, to freshen it up and make it lovely. Apologize for all the times the family rolled their eyes and said, 'not again'. She was expressing herself. Remember how those churches you*

were part of reinforced the message that women had to keep silent. That quenched your mum's spirit.

This isn't just about respect now. It's about being unable to communicate freely. I can see the flood of memories, Anya. Don't hurry now. Just bring them all to Me and release them. Speak forgiveness over every sad memory.

A little later . . .

Now Anya, you see how you share that legacy? You too, are bound in your expression, but I want to release you so that you can communicate honestly.

Please cover me, Lord, with Your protection. I place my whole family under Your care. It feels like I'm doing a dangerous thing. I am coming in Jesus' powerful name to set a captive free, and the captive is me.

I declare that Jesus died to set captives free. To mute tongues, he says 'speak,' to blind eyes, he says 'see,' to the dead, he says, 'arise!' So with faith in Him, I speak to my spirit, 'You are loosed in Jesus name. Be loosed. Be freed. Lips—be released to bless others and to speak respect for your husband.

In the Spirit I come and declare that my soul is *alive* unto God, my spirit will rejoice in God my Father and my lips will speak and sing His praises.

Anya, what you loose on earth, I loose in heaven. I release healing for your broken heart, liberty for your captive spirit, opening of the prison which has bound your expression. I send you my comfort—my Comforter.

I lift you from the ashes, my Daughter of Zion, and I give you beauty instead. I pour my joy into you, and—see that heavy spirit you wear? I slip my garment of praise over you instead.

You are a tree of righteousness. You will draw on living water; you will bring shade and bear fruit so that others can be nourished and blessed. This is not your doing. You are the planting of the Lord, and I will be glorified.

Lord, is this disrespect taken care of now?

Basically. You do respect Jeff. Now, walk in your freedom. You are free to show your respect. You have a policy with your children that if it's at all possible, you say, 'yes' to their requests. You can operate the same with Jeff, you know. Say 'yes' to Jeff whenever you can. You will enjoy unity with him and this will honor him.

Yes, it's okay now. The big things are done. Glorify me! I planted you, Anya. But you are a sapling. A little, fresh, green sapling. You're not a great tree yet! The journey is still starting, so go easy on yourself. You need to be staked—tied gently to me, so you will be protected, and so you will grow naturally. You will receive all the nourishment you need. New growth will appear in your life as the days go by.

Jeff will watch over you too. Your branches aren't strong enough for people to climb on or for children to hang off. Your trunk will not withstand too much shaking or carelessness. Your fruit is not ripe enough or plentiful enough to support a crowd.

But my little trees do grow quickly and naturally and beautifully. I love to bring heaven to earth. I want you and Jeff to be part of that.

Let me show you another tree. This one is beside my river; the river where I long to meet you. This tree bears fruit every month—whatever is right for the season. And the leaves are for the healing of the nations.

I finished the morning with praying the Daily Prayer for Freedom one more time.

'Heavenly Father, thank you for granting me every spiritual blessing in the heavenlies in Christ Jesus. I receive these blessings into my life today, and I ask the Holy Spirit to bring all those blessings into my life this day. Thank you for the blood of Jesus. Wash me once more with His blood from every sin and stain and evil device . . .

I call forth the kingdom of the Lord Jesus Christ this day throughout my home, my family, my life and my domain. I pray all this in the name of Jesus Christ with all glory and honor and thanks to Him.'

Day 24

Lord, as I go through each day I hear Your gentle voice and feel you nudging me into line with You. It's awesome. Thank you! But when Jeff talked about some of his latest ideas yesterday, I didn't have any sense that they were really from You. What do I do with that? I want to affirm him, but I don't want us to pour energy and time into initiatives that come to nothing. On the other hand, if these ideas come from You, I expect they will be maximally fruitful. That's why I feel like I need to be sure.

Anya, you have brought your questions to me. Thank you. But now, start your day in worship. Read a Psalm to me. Praise me and place your trust in me for this day.

Too soon the children will wake, and this time will end. Use it to love me and to receive my love for you.

Day 25

Dear Lord, this is difficult. I can see that You are at work in me and in Jeff and in our marriage. I just didn't realize how tender I still am—even where You've healed the wound, it still feels tender sometimes.

> *You need me for your healing, Anya, but you need me to support and guide you day by day as well.*

He brought it up, Lord. I didn't. He saw that book, '*Captivating*,' beside my bed and asked if I'd read it, if anything in it had made a difference to me. I knew right away that this was a bare-your-soul moment. I told him that I suspect that book, and particularly that prayer of freedom I've been praying to You . . . saved my life. I know how far down I was, Lord. I can't begin to describe how You've rescued me. And Jeff was interested, so I tried to tell him.

> *It didn't end well.*

No, it didn't. I wanted to show him how reading that book

prompted me to write out my conversation with You. He wanted to see it. So I offered to show him these journals. *Oh God.* These journals aren't just a window into my soul. They're throw-the-whole-door-open access to my soul. I was believing You had healed me enough to do that.

> *I love your courage. You did an amazing thing, inviting Jeff into your life like that.*

> *Tell me what you desired. Lay out your disappointment before me.*

I hoped he'd realize what a treasure this time with You has been—how precious You have become to me, and how sacred this feels. I guess I expected he'd take it and read it slowly and carefully.

> *And then he asked something of you. He asked you to read it to him. Not the whole book, Anya. Just a sentence or two.*

Yes, and I freaked out. It was as if him reading my words wasn't being vulnerable enough. Now he wanted me to sit there and read it aloud?

> *Anya, you need to listen to me carefully now. I have some things to say to you. Will you pray now for grace to receive my words?*

Yes Lord. I've brought you my dilemma. My frustration. Now I lay it down. Search me and know me, reveal to me what is not pleasing to you . . . grant me grace to receive Your words and to deeply and truly repent.

These are the two things I want to say:

First, you should have brought your need for affirmation to me alone. You looked to Jeff when you should have looked to me. I would have whispered into your ear 'Yes! You can do this! It's only a few sentences and I will help you.'

I would have assured you that your voice is important and that I would guard and hold your soul even as it trembles.

I see now. I'm sorry Lord. Please keep this lesson in my heart. If I had come to you earlier in the day, and really been filled by Your Spirit, I would have turned my ear to your voice before I ruined that moment. I responded independently of You and I'm sorry . . .

The second thing is this, Anya. It comes up often, but now is the time to deal with it.

You have a spirit of distrust, which leads you to fear Jeff and to mistake his heart for you. If you trust in his love for you, you can rest in it and avoid always questioning his motives. You will be able to believe the best of him, and stop making the wrong assumptions.

Is this just a small, isolated spirit?

It's easily dealt with, but no, it's not so small, though it has kept a low profile.

And now, this spirit of distrust has a companion, called Blame.

Thank you, Lord, for showing me this. And for confidence to release myself from their influence. Please help me now.

In Jesus name and authority, I name this spirit of Distrust in my life. I confess that I have listened to his lies and lived by its assumptions. I ask You, Lord to forgive me. I declare that Christ is worthy of my trust. He empowers me to trust and not to be afraid. He lived a life of trust and my life is hidden in His.

So now, I address you, spirit of Distrust. Your time with me is up. You have placed lying thoughts and suggestions in my mind for too long. Your father is a liar. I now renounce your claim to my life. I command you to remove every attachment you have on me. In Jesus' precious name, I command you to let go of me completely.

Spirit of Blame—you have no place in me now. I have long believed the worst of Jeff, and have blamed him for anything and everything. I declare that blame has no place in a child of God. You too, must follow Distrust. You must let go of me.

In Jesus' name, I bind Blame and Distrust together. Go and present yourselves before the Lord, and do as He commands, never to return. In Jesus' name, I cast you out.

Now, Anya, place my cross, my finished work of love, between you and Jeff . . .

I now bring the cross of Christ between me and Jeff. Distrust and blame must bow at the cross. Only kindness and truth and love can pass between us.

Lastly, Anya, before we go into this day . . . you asked me about Jeff's idea. You didn't trust that he got the idea from me. You misread his heart and accused him of caring more for his ideas that for you. That was a lie, and I'm sorry you believed it. But now, Distrust is gone, and so is Blame. Here's a verse is for you:

THE LORD OF HEAVEN'S ARMIES IS A WONDERFUL TEACHER, AND HE GIVES THE FARMER GREAT WISDOM.   ISAIAH 28:29 NLT

I am both a warrior and a teacher, Anya. When Jeff and I were fighting for your financial freedom, I also taught him. I gave him specific details. Just as I give the farmer specific wisdom for his field, even though he has grown up on the land and 'should' know what to do, so I gave Jeff, who is a businessman, and a good one too, great wisdom. His ideas came from me. Please don't separate my wisdom and my warfare. As I command heaven's armies, I also instruct my people.

Thank you, Lord. I get it now.

Can I ask you today for some wisdom of my own? I need to know how our children should be educated here in Turkey.

We had enrolled our children in a Turkish-speaking school soon after we arrived. We'd got through the first weeks, all of us sobbing wrecks when the school van pulled up outside out home with its blacked-out windows, and the supervisor who stepped out all covered up in a trench coat and headscarf and not speaking a word of

English, took our girls hands, hustled them inside and slammed the door as the van pulled off down the street. But we'd got used to the system, and the girls were doing well in preschool. At least, so we thought. But that's another story.

The boys were on their primary school campus were quickly picking up the language. But once we picked up on issues like the huge porn culture, the horror movies being shown in lunch hours, the animosity our boys experienced, being the only foreigners most the other kids had ever known, and the lack of space for any personal opinion or expression, we knew something had to change. It was becoming clear that Turkish school system was not going to prepare our children adequately for life outside of Turkey.

The trouble was, there weren't many options. We needed a solution from God.

Day 26

(otherwise known as the day Anya decided to color her hair)

I started life as blonde as a kid can get, and had lived thirty-seven years without coloring my hair. Not a streak, not a highlight, not a wash—nothing. But I'd always wondered what I'd look like if I were a rich, dark brown, so in a regrettable moment at the grocery store, I bought a pack of hair dye, walked back down the hill to our home, went into the bathroom and went to work.

Thus began one of the most traumatic days of my life. First, the color looked ridiculous on me. My skin tone suddenly looked terrible, my clothes clashed, I could barely recognize the person in the mirror, and worst of all, I didn't look like the mother of my four blonde children anymore. The whole thing needed rectifying fast.

Only, changing from blonde to dark brown is one thing. Changing it back is another. Jeff ran back up the road and purchased a nice pack of golden blonde dye, similar to my natural color. Perfect, I thought—until I actually applied it. Turns out that blonde on top of dark brown leads to bright orange. Not auburn, or any shade thereof. Just poster-paint orange. There was no way I could leave the house.

After an extensive and demoralizing internet search, we realized there was no way forward except to remove every ounce of color and start again, and even then, the warnings and disclaimers came thick and fast. But desperation had taken hold; I could not very well stay housebound for the next six months, and I wasn't sure that I could find a blonde wig in Turkey if we resorted to the shave-it-all-off option.

So Jeff, in his kindness, went back to the store and purchased our third and fourth packs of hair dye—straight peroxide, and yet another round of blonde.

The peroxide worked. As in, everyone in the family took one look at their me and hid their faces. Liberty burst into tears on the spot, which is understandable. Her mother looked like a ghost. It turns out that being teased for having white hair as a kid was nothing. *This* was white. Pure white, with not a drop of tint, and looking in the mirror left me traumatized.

Jeff was reassuring. 'We're not finished yet. Now let's put your proper color back in,' he said, always the man with a plan. For this to end well, we needed to finish the job. And, *it worked*. Four hours after that fateful decision, I vaguely resembled the Anya I had always been. I brewed a pot of tea, the whole family sat on the couch, wrapping our arms around each other in a great bundle of love and relief, and eventually I even stopped trembling.

Having never used chemicals on my hair before, I hadn't counted on how much damage the whole process had done. Now my hair was literally brittle. But I could work with that. Most importantly, life could go on.

Father, that was one mean attack on me, wasn't it?

Yes, it sure was. But see how much I love you! Satan knows how to hurt you. But even he was surprised at how deeply that reached. You feeling beautiful is important, Anya. It's important to me.

It was just so hard, when You have done so much to heal me and give me hope and peace. It was like we'd finished another stage of the journey. I think it hurt because I tried to make myself lovely, and then I was discontent with the look, and didn't feel like myself at all, and then, oh God, that orange! I've never looked so horrendous. And it seemed there was no way to fix it.

I heard the devil whisper, '*see, it doesn't matter what God has done, you're still only one mistake away from a meltdown. You're only as good as your looks. If I make you ugly, ashamed, a joke—if I show what a try-hard you are—it will all come to nothing. In the end, it's not about your soul. It's all about externals, your beauty, and now you have none.*'

Dear God, I know it was him, his final onslaught, but I hate that I co-operated with him. Why didn't I ask You before I blundered in and ruined myself?

Why did Lazarus die?

Oh! You wanted to show Your love and power. To glorify yourself.

Yes. And I let you get to that point. I allowed Satan to lay his hand on your most tender issue. I wanted to have this final victory so you would know once and for all that I love you, that you're worth it, and that I am your Healer and Defender.

I saw how much Jeff *cared* about me too. He felt for me and rose up for me. He knew how to fix it, and I *trusted him*! I'm so glad I didn't run off to some Turkish hairdresser in a panic. It was just up to us.

Exactly. From now on, you shall know that I have healed another wound. Your sadness and striving and self-consciousness is dealt with. It's been healed by love. When I see you, I see beauty.

Thank you. I *feel* lovely—probably for the first time in my life, I *feel* lovely even without trying. You and Jeff are very, very kind.

Day 27

Yesterday we went shopping. I had never liked shopping, but we came across some amazing sales, and I do love a bargain. That's when I noticed the difference in me. As I tried on new clothes, I saw myself in a whole new way. Not only did it feel like fun to be shopping, but I felt beautiful when I looked in the mirror!

Lord, it's lovely to wake up each day to *You*! I still can't believe how, when I went into shops yesterday with Jeff, every piece of clothing I tried looked *lovely* on me. Wow, I never expected You to make this so easy, Lord.

And this morning when we woke, we made love to each other and afterwards I didn't feel crabby. Thank you, Lord. Until now, I've had to battle this horrible mean spirit towards Jeff—not so much while we're enjoying each other—but afterwards. I know Lord, that we still have more freedom to experience and receive from You in this area, but I just want to thank you that you have released me from the inner ugliness I have always felt afterwards . . .

Good morning to you too, my dear one!

I heard you whisper how much you hope my work in you doesn't end here. Today, Anya, when I say, 'Good morning' to you, I want you to know that, in Me, you are being greeted into the morning of your life. I have awakened you. This is the day I have made. Rejoice and be glad in it. Walk gently with me. This is only the beginning.

That's funny, because I've always feared dying young. I've just expected it. My Nana lost her mind so early; my granddad died so young. I've never been able to picture a long, healthy life. When Jeff prayed that for me last night—prayed that I'd live to see my children's children—my spirit said, *Yes!*

Life in its fullness is mine to give Anya. Walk with me.

Lord, I love You. Thank you for your amazing Son. I love that he knows, not just the burden of shame and sadness and sin, but he also knows what it's like to be set free—free from death, free from all the brokenness he lived amongst. I wish I had the words to tell Him what that means to me. My words don't do You justice. Even my thoughts of You still fall short of the honor I'd like to give You. Please set my spirit free to praise You more fully.

Dear Lord, I'm learning so much about You. I've also noticed what a huge difference it makes when I start the day with that prayer. I don't feel like I'm trapped in whatever circumstance that day brings. I remember my authority in You, and everything is, well . . . a lot better.

One thing about yesterday bothers me though. I went and bought those clothes that made me feel lovely, but on the way home, I realized I'd spent too much money this week. It dawned on me that perhaps You just wanted to show me my beauty and convince me of Your love for me, but I ended up overreacting and buying the lot. I grabbed a few too many bargains, didn't I? Sorry, Lord.

> *I understand. Grabbing is a problem for you, and we should talk that through.*

> *Remember the tourists that you saw in Istanbul?*

Yes. They come to Turkey and stay in lovely all-inclusive hotels. I've watched them when they come to the buffet. They load their plates like gluttons. They don't go back and forth, like most people do. They load up three or four plates right away as if they're scared they might miss out. I figure they can't shake the old-era mindset that next time they look there might be nothing left.

> *Now consider your past. Don't get too specific. Just see if you have anything in common with those tourists.*

Well, that's easy Lord. For years my family only just had enough. There were no guarantees for tomorrow, especially when we were in Canada and Albania. Even before that, it never felt as if there was enough to make treats *feel* like treats, or splurges *feel* special. It's as if splurges were fun in the moment, but then left us feeling guilty.

Now I want to surprise you with delight. List your most extravagant memories. See how much you've been given. See that you have had anything but a sparse life.

I remembered going to the theatre in London with my mum, and to the Queensland Performing Arts Center with my dad to watch *Joseph and the Amazing Technicolor Dreamcoat.* We had farm holidays in New Zealand and camping holidays and trips to the snow. There was our family's Sunday lunch tradition at the Leviathan Hotel in Dunedin, breakfasts at the Heritage Hotel in Brisbane, and a wonderful few days in Hawaii and Disneyland.

I had visited Hyde Park and Buckingham Palace and Covent Garden; we'd explored mountains in Switzerland and castles in Scotland, we'd toured Oxford and Stonehenge and Bath. I'd stayed in the Black Forest and taken trips to Albania and Greece.

I remembered the gifts my parents had bought me along the way—a garnet ring for my graduation from university, a gold necklace on the ferry between Italy and Greece, and my first car when I started university. There had been violin lessons and piano lessons and a year of education at a private high school and four years' worth of university fees all paid upfront. . .

Wow, that was a reality check! I realize, Lord, that my family probably never felt like they could afford all this, but they made it happen anyway and they are now wonderful memories. I've had anything but a scarce life. Thank you for it all.

And that only covers the years before you were married.

It would look the same if we listed all Jeff and you have done and enjoyed together.

What do I do with this?

You recognize that none of these wonderful gifts led to lack. You didn't miss out on what you needed because of them. Perhaps you just missed being thankful and really enjoying them with a trust that all would be well the day after, the month after, and the year after . . . Look at how your Father loved you and gave you special treats as well as supplying all your needs.

I don't want to feel guilty when I enjoy Your gifts. But I also don't want to grab at things. If I really trusted that You will always provide our needs, I could say *no* more. Please reveal the roots and weeds, the strongholds perhaps . . . the real issues of my heart. I'd like You to heal me in this area if you're willing and the time is right.

We'll get there. But today, Jeff and I have teamed up to give you a chance to learn Turkish. Don't squander this gift. Enjoy it. There will be another time for all the other concerns you have.

Day 28

Lord, I want to ask you, is there some key that will unlock my language-learning? Do I have to just work harder and harder until I get it, or is there some way You want to meet me in this?

Anya, pray that prayer again. See how I guide you.

Oh Lord, this is all relevant. I bring it all to you with regard to learning Turkish.

Focus on the agreements you have made with the enemy—the things you have said, that he has been happy to heartily endorse and enforce. You've said, 'I'm not young anymore. I was good at languages when I was young.' You've said things like, 'I can't remember anything' and 'I can't think fast enough to respond in Turkish.'

You keep talking about how the language is 'çok zor, so hard.' And everyone around you nods, but that's the way it is, Anya. You're focusing on how difficult it is.

You've also convinced yourself that you can live in Turkey and be effective without learning the language. You say that you don't have time or that everything else will suffer if you make this a priority. It's all a lot of excuses, Anya.

You need to repent. These attitudes and words are not from me. Your enemy who wants to close your mouth and keep you from speaking Turkish has told you all these lies. You agreed with him, and spoke accordingly. Then he, in turn, added his agreement, and now you're stuck.

Renounce your words. Deny them any claim on your life. Call each of them a lie. Then speak aloud the truth that is in Christ Jesus.

Okay.

I now address the lie that I have spoken, that I used to be good at languages but I am not anymore. I declare that this comes from the father of lies, and not from my Father. I now renounce this lie, and deny it any claim on my life or language-learning. I receive the promise of Christ that he will renew my youth, and I thank Him that he has gifted me with the ability to learn this language at this stage in my life.

I address the lie that 'I can't remember anything.' This, too, is from Satan, and so I annul his words and renounce them in Jesus name. I retract my agreement and instead lay claim to the truth, that those who are in Christ can open their mouths and that the Holy Spirit can bring words to my

memory, just as He brings the words of Christ to my memory.

I address the lie that 'I can't think quickly enough to respond . . .' I annul this agreement In Jesus' name. The truth I take is that I can open my mouth, and He, my God, will fill it.

I address the lie that this language is very difficult. I renounce the words, 'çok zor.' My God can change mountains in to plains. He can remove mountains, in fact. This is the truth I claim and lay hold of as I approach language-learning, and I thank God for his mighty power and His willingness to remove every difficulty and hindrance.

I now confront the lie from Satan which I have foolishly agreed with, that I can live in Turkey without learning Turkish. I repent of this lie, which hurts me and dishonors and robs the precious people among whom I live. I declare that I want to learn Turkish. God communicates with me in ways I am able to understand, and I will do the same with the people in my life.

I come in Jesus' name to renounce the lie, and my agreement with it, that I do not have the time to learn Turkish, and that other things will suffer if I do. I reject this lie, and stand firm in Christ, who in a moment, created life from nothing, called forth the dead, brought hope to the hopeless. I stand in

Jesus, who, in three years, showed the way into the Kingdom—He who in one dark day, bore away the sin of the world. He is not limited by time and neither am I.

I cling to Him who left nothing neglected. He who ministered to multitudes, yet still communed long with His Father. I trust in Him who offered the same reward to those who labored all day as to those who labored for just one hour.

Finally, I repent of the lie that I tried but have now lost confidence to speak in Turkish. Satan wants this to be all about me, but I affirm that God is the Hero of this story, and I belong to Him. My confidence is in Him. Today I gratefully take up the confidence I need to speak. In Christ, I am bold. He gives me courage. He Himself is my confidence, and He is as present as ever!

Day 29

Lord, it's as if, just when I determine to put language first, everything else presses in. I know You've called me to lead this Foreigner's Working Group, but Lord, how do I manage the huge list of things I should do?

> *You need to ask me about everything, Anya. Every email, phone call, appointment, letter, meeting—you need to see my nod of approval before you act. I'll keep it all in its place. Your need is to look to me. It's coming so fast, in fact, that you'll need to fix your eyes on me. Okay?*

Day 30

Lord, one more thing. When I read '*Captivating*,' Stasi mentioned episodes where she got dizzy. She realized that it was some form of spiritual attack, that it was not that it was not just a natural or normal thing and she rebuked the dizziness. The whole thing got worse and more frequent, but she kept at it until one day, it just left her. The dizzy spells stopped. I feel the same with bouts of exhaustion. They hit me so randomly. It's been worse since I started focusing on Turkish.

I love how my people share their stories and share their experiences. It's another way you can hear me speak. I imprinted that testimony on you because it is for you! You're right. A spirit of exhaustion trails you, attacking you as you go through your day. Resist it. Resist the devil and he will, eventually, flee from you.

Fight this battle. It may get worse before we win the victory, but you are up for this.

Every time you sense this exhaustion coming over you, stand firm in my authority—I who never tire or grow weary—rebuke it, and command it to leave. The important thing is to do this as soon as you come under attack.

Don't give in and lie down or close your eyes, or you'll forget to fight. You might feel a little better after a sleep, but the enemy will chuckle and I you will not have the victory we want here. So be fast and decisive, stand confidently in your authority, and determine to keep it up until this affliction is past. If your body feels tired, or even if your mind feels exhausted while you study language—resist. Command tiredness to leave you.

My name is a strong tower. The righteous run to it, and they are saved. So, resist in my name, and watch for your deliverance.

Day 31

Hear my cry, O God; attend to my prayer.
From the ends of the earth I will cry to you,
When my heart is overwhelmed, Lead me to the
rock that is higher than I . . . Psalm 61:1,2

Truly my soul silently waits before God
From Him comes my salvation. Psalm 62:1

Day 32

Lord, I don't know if I was fully awake, or asleep last night when those thoughts—that picture—entered my mind. I wondered if you were giving me some insight into our work here, but how do I know if it was even from you?

It was the closest thing I'd ever had to a vision.

I saw a gate opening onto a wide, tree-lined pavement. I knew the place. To the left of the pavement, was the municipality building where my volunteer working group and the city officials had our offices.

On the opposite side of the path, I saw the little company Jeff and I had brought to Turkey. I had often wondered why our company had never been given any city council work, despite the obvious need for our services.

Now I could see that some spirit or spirits were positioned between the two entities. Instinctively I knew that one was a spirit of Apathy. I wasn't sure if there was another spirit also. The word *'summon'* came to my mind, along with the knowledge that the cross of Jesus should be the only thing between our company and the city council.

It was from me, Anya. When you woke this morning, this vision was still clear to you. I do not let my words be lost. And it was not from the enemy, because the vision holds the key to blessing—and he never desires your blessing.

How do I know it's not just my imagination?

For a long time, you were told not to trust your feelings. Perhaps you think of imagination in the same way. As if the only part of you I work through is your mind.

Well, that is far from the truth. I redeemed you, spirit, soul, mind and body.

You have been praying, 'I give you my spirit, soul, mind and body.' Anya, there amongst it all is your imagination. In many languages and cultures, there is no difference between one's 'soul' and one's 'imagination.' So yes, in part, it was your imagination, your mind turning ideas and dreams into pictures—and yes, it was all from me.

I trust you, Lord, and I'm learning to trust myself too. You really do fill my being. I don't need to doubt or be afraid.

Let's complete the picture. There are two spirits, both blocking your way. You know they need your editing and writing services. One spirit is Apathy. Apathy makes these people believe that the standard of English in their publications doesn't really matter. And the other spirit is Ignorance— keeping these influential people from even knowing how atrocious their

English translations are. This has been affirmed to you by three different people in the last two days.

It was true. I had sat down with some trusted local friends who knew the culture and wanted our company to succeed. All three, independently of each other, had mentioned, in one way or another, these two issues, and all had conveyed the opinion that there was not a lot we could do to change either the apathy or the ignorance in our city.

Lord, how do I deal with these spirits? I feel like they're not really fighting against me, or terribly bothered about me. They seem more concerned with guarding their buildings and territory—the city council and municipality.

Exactly.

So how do I proceed? I don't feel inclined to pick a fight with spirits who are not aggressively against me. It's like they're just there, doing their job.

Yes. Their job is to keep blessing out. To guard. Satan does not desire the blessing of this institution, or this city. But I do, and so do you. I brought you here to open the door for my blessing on this city I love. And no, I do not want you to pick the fight. This is not just about you and your family and your business. It's about my glory and my kingdom. This time, you are to stand in my authority and summon my angels to fight against Apathy and Ignorance and to release this city from their control.

That was the reason for the word 'summon?'

Yes.

I haven't done this before.

> *No, but each day you have been praying, 'Father, thank you for your angels. I summon them in the authority of Jesus Christ and release them to war for me and my household . . .'*

Do I just say something similar, but about my company and the city council?

> *Yes. There is no formula. You may use your own words. It's your words, spoken in my authority that counts. And Anya?*

Yes?

> *I love to summon my angels. I chose not to summon them when I was dying on the cross, so that we could have moments like this—moments where my triumph is seen. Because I did not call them to release me from death, you can now summon them for a deliverance such as this. I am excited by the thought.*

I loved that I was being called to intercede for something bigger than myself. It had taken a great deal of breakthrough to get to this point, and now God was entrusting me to stand in the gap for our city. I sensed His excitement, and felt that excitement within me too. It was reassuring that I couldn't get it wrong, that I was being set up to win a victory for this city God had brought us to. I opened my mouth and began speaking . . .

Today I stand in the name of Christ Jesus and in the authority of my role in the city council and my relationship with the city council and the municipality.

I ask You, Father to protect me and all I love, including those who work at these organizations. And now I stand aside, and, in the name of the Lord Jesus I summon the angels of God's choice to fight against Apathy and Ignorance as they guard the way to the city council and municipality and cultural congress in this city.

I declare to the angels of God that these two enemy spirits are blocking the path of blessing for this city and for my company. This is the intention of the enemy. But I declare that God is *for* this city. He desires the blessing of this city and of my family, as well as many others. There is more at stake than meets the eye. Angels of God—fight for your Creator's glory. Fight until the enemy is fully subdued, disarmed and put to flight.

You are angels of light. You are His warriors. You have been selected from the heavenly host for this fight and for this victory. In Jesus' authority and according to His directive, I now release you to war against the spirits of Ignorance and Apathy in this place. In His name, be victorious!

Anya, this feels new to you. You are wondering if there will be any victory.

You have felt this way after every fight, but don't heed those thoughts. Remember this verse:

IF GOD IS FOR US, WHO CAN BE AGAINST US? HE WHO DID NOT SPARE HIS OWN SON, HOW SHALL HE NOT, WITH HIM, GIVE US ALL THINGS? ROMANS 8:31-32

Put your trust in me again.

Lord, what's this? It's as if a huge wave of loneliness has swept over me. I'm doing this with You, I know—it doesn't make sense—but this lonely feeling that has come upon me is so *real*. It feels *physical*, Lord, like I can't breathe, like a knot in my stomach. Jeff asked me what was wrong and I couldn't answer. How do I put the last month into words? You're taking me to a whole other level and it's all so new.

This is another attack on you, Anya. It's not the way it feels. Draw near to me, and resist the devil. When he flees, the loneliness will flee, and you will have Me. I will comfort you by my Holy Spirit. But Anya, my angels are warring for more than just your future. The city's prosperity is at stake.

That afternoon, a city council election was to be held to decide whether the President, a man I worked closely with, would retain his position for another term. An alternative candidate had been nominated as well, a man known for his feistiness and hardline stance on many issues. I had been invited to the meeting, and as representative of my working group, I would have the right to vote.

I knew, however, that the outcome needed to be decided in the heavenlies before we even got to the meeting. And so I left the house an hour earlier than I'd planned, and, arriving at the Congress Center precinct, I continued spurring on the angels of God . . .

> *You are looking on today. Cheer, Anya. Speak promises of victory. Sing songs of worship and deliverance. The battle has begun, but today is not a day for rest. The angels I sent out are accustomed to hearing praise. Songs of deliverance spur them on.*

Lord Jesus, would you send forth your singing, praising Host? Please release them today to rejoice and clap and declare Your supremacy over this city. Would you let your warring angels hear heaven's praises as they fight, not to distract them, but to bolster their resolve? To spur them on to quicker, more spectacular victory?

Let our enemies hear the sounds of heaven's triumph. Let them hear the name of the Son of God, Captain of the Angel Armies, and let them shrink back and retreat. I join your choir, your ministers, those who do Your will.

Having summoned not only angels to fight, but a host of angels to praise the Lord in their hearing, I knew I was to join in song as well. Walking the perimeter of the park, I sang under my breath, worshipping God, and as I did so, it felt as if I were calling on even more angels to join in . . .

'How great is our God, sing with me, how great is our God. And all will see how great—how great, is our God.'

Lord, this is so unusual. I have a very strong sense that I can't do this alone—that I shouldn't. But who else is there?

Tell Jeff. He'll cover you and rise up for you. Ask for his help.

I called Jeff and told him what I was doing. For the next forty minutes, I kept praising. I felt as if the angels of God were winning so long as I kept worshipping. And then, just as clearly as I had sensed the need to call this battle to begin, I knew it was over. The apathy and ignorance that had influenced our city were gone, and as I entered the Congress Center and took my place in the special election meeting, I knew the outcome had already been decided. . .

Day 33

Father, Jeff was amazing yesterday. He took me seriously. He knew exactly what to say. He prayed for me and confirmed much of what You've said. He agrees that this is not just about our company—it's the key to our city, the government and even to the success of our friends here. It's time, Lord. This combination of ignorance and apathy is everywhere. People just shrug and say, 'This is Turkey . . .' They're so resigned. No sense of personal responsibility and initiative to change. I stand against those words '*This is Turkey,*' because it's not the Turkey You desire. If my child was ignorant and apathetic, I would not shrug and just say, 'Well, that's my son.' I'd fight for him. I'd pray against it until he came alive.

> *Yes—we have a big job on our hands. Every time you hear those words, say, 'I reject that. I send those words back to where they came from.'* I will honor that. Let's speak hope and blessing over this place.

Okay.

Lord, when I prayed this morning, the word 'anointed' stood

out. 'Anoint me for all of my life and work and calling . . .'

When this city cracks and those two spirits are gone for good, I need to be ready to move in, however you show me. Please Lord, anoint me for all my life and work and calling.

I have set you apart for some special privileges and tasks. When the time is right, I will anoint you for that.

Day 34

Lord, to be honest, I'm overwhelmed. I want to pray more. I have a whole list of things on my heart for the advance of Your kingdom, and yet, realistically, the housework keeps piling up, I have a huge amount of work to do for the city council, my schedule is packed with people-appointments and we have all our dear friends and family back home in Australia that I want to keep in touch with. There are constant visitors to our home and there's our four darling children plus another two that I am now about to start homeschooling several days a week. I should be learning Turkish. And I'm tired.

Lord, I get up early to spend these hours with you, but how long can I keep this up?

Turn to that daily prayer, Anya, and read it to Me.

Oh! 'My dear Lord Jesus. I come to you now to be *restored* in you . . .' Wow! This time is not making me tired. This time with You is restorative.

Yes. And if you live by my Spirit, you will hear me calling you to rest or to activity or to worship . . . and you will not be overwhelmed. When it feels like your days are overtaking you, look to me. Turn your eyes upon me. Let me guide you through the hours. Do not do everything that comes into your head, or you will be led by your flesh. Do what I place in your spirit. Follow my gentle prompts. And if you are not sure, ask me.

Lord, when I woke this morning, that girl I met from Iran came to mind. She's going back home very soon and I never got the chance to meet up properly with her. It sounds pointless to try and fit her in now—besides, today I have an editing job for the city council, and school things to sort through. And piles of laundry.

Just send her a text message or call her . . . I'll take it from there.

Okay. And Lord? Another friend offered to come and set up the schoolroom and I feel all worried about what she's going to do. I want it to still feel like it's my home, not someone else's idea of a classroom. I know it's petty, but . . .

Anya, give her space to do her thing. Be honest if you don't like something. But remember that you gave her freedom.

I WILL PRAISE THE NAME OF GOD WITH A SONG, AND WILL MAGNIFY HIM WITH THANKSGIVING. THIS ALSO SHALL PLEASE THE LORD BETTER THAN AN OX OR BULL. PSALM 69:30-31

You are not looking for a sign of strength or for a showy sacrifice from me today, are You, Lord? It's enough if I love and worship You, and give thanks as I go.

Day 34

Yes. I love you. Go into the day in peace. My peace I give to you.

Day 35

Thank you, Lord. You did it! My friend came and got us all organized, and Lord, she was such a blessing. She made the schoolroom look lovely, and she sorted through everything so beautifully. You helped us, and we didn't get overwhelmed, and I'm so excited with Your plans for our kids' schooling.

And when I finally tracked Leila down, she said she could meet me tomorrow. That's so much easier for me, Lord. Thank you. I assume we should ask her to represent our company in Iran. Is that why You are bringing us together at the last minute?

Day 36

Lord, this confuses me. When Jeff woke up this morning, he said he had prayed about Leila last night, and it was as though heaven was screaming not to touch this girl. That we must not ask her to work for us. Lord, why? Why does so much about this company seem to be what *not* to do? We thought the idea was from You . . .

Now all I can think is that it's not worth taking two buses and heading out for half a day if we don't even have a job to offer her.

> *Anya, though this confused you for a while, I heard you pray to me, and I watched you choose to trust Jeff. In that, you trusted me. Now go. Meet Leila. You can see how the enemy is trying to stop this from happening. The children are a bit ratty. The housework is getting to you. Just walk out the door and go meet her.*

Lord Jesus, I think You are telling me that Leila has something to give me. That it was never about what we could do for her.

Yes, now you've got it.

Lord, I open my life to You—to receive from Leila all You have for me. Please unite our spirits. Let us experience a connection in that is from You. In Jesus' name, I forbid any enemy spirits from interfering in our time together, and I release heaven's blessings . . .

Day 37

Meeting with Leila, the young woman from Iran, absolutely blew my mind. She told me her story—how her family broke down, how she become ill and the doctors could not figure out what was wrong, how in desperation her mother took her to a little church in Tehran, and how as the pastor there prayed for her, Jesus came stood over her, spoke to her and healed her.

I heard what a tough time she's had here in Turkey. She's going home tomorrow, because the Lord told her she was to strengthen her own people and be a voice for Him in her country. 'Besides', she said, 'it's as if the sky above Turkey is closed, but above Iran, it's wide open.'

I love when God messes with my mind. I'd known Turkey was a tough gig spiritually, but to hear that even Iran was easy compared to this, found me nodding in agreement and laughing at the absurdity of the whole thing. 'Spiritually-speaking', Leila assured me, 'Iran is free and thriving.' 'Here in Turkey', she said, 'the heavens are shut. It's hard to even pray.'

Wow, Lord, listening to that girl makes me adore You. I resonated with her as soon as she started talking. When she told me how You miraculously gave her the ability to speak flawless Turkish in just three months, it blew me away. I didn't realize how much I'm longing for the miraculous. I want a language-testimony like that too!

God had spoken to me that he would give me the ability to speak Turkish through other people. I assumed He meant the people who had offered to teach me. But I knew that even if we stayed in Turkey for another three years, there was no way I could devote the time it would take to acquire the language simply by study and practice.

Right before we said goodbye, Leila asked if I wanted to be able to speak Turkish. Without even thinking, I said 'of course!' Then she took my hand, laid another hand on my head and prayed that I would receive the gift she had received. She said God's gifts were for passing on. Then she assured me that in a very short time I would be speaking Turkish.

I surprised you, didn't I?

Yes, for sure. I wish I'd got to know her earlier. Her courage as she leaves tonight to return to Iran and her confidence that You will keep her despite the threat to her life is astounding. I thought I was going to bless her, but I was the one who received the blessing. Thank you, Father.

Day 38

Lord, when I was feeling desperate, I craved You. You led me and answered me as I poured out my heart to you. You met me in that, Lord. My soul was dead and You brought it to life. It was wonderful.

Right now, I don't feel desperate. There are all sorts of things I want to bring to You but none of it feels urgent. And I'm tired, so I'm not getting up as early in the morning to come into Your presence. Then when I pray anyway, I don't know where to start. Is it possible to experience the warmth of Your love *every* day?

I love your question! Were all David's Psalms desperate?

No. Many were. The others were full of . . . praise. Praise and quiet requests.

That's right. When you are not engaging in battles or fleeing for refuge from the harshness of life—you praise. Worship me. Remember all I have done. Sing of my grace and compassion, how slow to anger I am, how great in mercy. I will meet you there. And Anya?

Yes?

I want you to know that, however much you enjoyed my love when you came to me for deliverance and healing and help . . . it will be vastly overwhelmed by what you will experience of me when you come to worship.

Are you going to open up a whole new world to me?

In a way. All your worship of me has been sweet. But there is a sense of intimacy in your worship you haven't experienced yet, and it will thrill your heart. Remember I said to you that your healing and freedom was not the end-point of your journey. It is only the beginning.

It really is like new birth, isn't it, God? '*Born Again*' so perfectly describes what You've done for me! I never imagined that I could feel so alive.

It was the day I had broken down the last big stronghold. I felt like a weight I didn't even know I was carrying—a weight that had been there all my life—was lifted off me. Suddenly I felt like I was taking my first breath of spiritual air.

Though I had 'accepted Jesus' as a four-year-old girl, I now found myself on the other side of the world, at the age of thirty-seven, saying, 'Oh God, is this what it *feels like* to be born again?!'

It was a holy moment, and tears of joy and relief flooded down my cheeks.

PART THREE

Ramadan had ended a few days earlier, but I wasn't ready to stop. I sensed God was calling me to new levels of worship, and though I had no idea where that would lead, I was beginning to look outside myself and feel God's heart for the people and world around me. What I didn't know was that by the end of the month, I would experience one of my most profound God-moments yet.

Day 39

Dear Lord, I'm overwhelmed. You're calling me to worship You, but I need to make some urgent decisions. I'm leading this working group, Lord, and there's an incredible level of momentum right now, which is great, but I can hardly keep up with it all. Lord, I need someone to head up the online language training project we've proposed, and I'm not sure who should do that. I know I need to hear a fresh word from You about this city and my work at the city council. I want to pray over our friendships, and my children all have issues I need to work through with You. And there are still areas in my own life I'm asking You to heal.

I feel stretched in too many directions, Father, and I still get these huge bouts of tiredness whenever I sit down with You. I don't have the self-discipline for this—the sort of self-discipline that can say 'not now' to the to-do list in my mind so that I can worship You.

Anya, you don't need to be more disciplined. Self-control can be something you try to acquire, or it can be the outcome of having my Spirit with you.

You can cut through all this concern, all the clutter in your mind . . . by simply being filled with Me—with my Spirit. Don't sit there trying to put everything in its place, or trying to prioritize. Be filled with the Spirit today. Start with that Prayer for Freedom once again.

I prayed again.

'*Holy and victorious Trinity, you alone are worthy of all my worship . . .*'

The call I sensed to worship the Lord was strong, but the list of issues to sort through in my mind kept pushing their way to the front. Choosing to worship in this moment felt close to impossible.

And then I prayed this phrase: '*I take my place in your ascension. . .*'

Suddenly I pictured cutting through this earthly realm and rising above it all, into a realm where worship is continual and natural.

Lord, I love to come here, to Your presence; I take my place here with You, Lord Jesus—ascended, loved and honored. This is where You want me to dwell. I am raised with You, Lord Jesus, seated with You . . .

'*Holy Spirit, apply to me all the fullness of the work of the ascension of Jesus Christ for me. I receive it with thanks, and give it total claim to my life. . .*'

Anya, look what you prayed. When you take your place in my ascension, worship will be natural. You are with Me today, enfolded in this union— the three of Us . . . and you! And as for all those 'things of earth' that caused you to be overwhelmed? Watch what happens when you pray, 'Holy Spirit, I sincerely receive You as my Counsellor.'

It's still hazy Lord, but I'm beginning to glimpse how this works.

'Fill me afresh, Blessed Holy Spirit. . .'

Oh, Lord, I need You. I can't lead these people You've given me or keep up with what You're doing here in Turkey in my own strength. Living out of Your presence needs to become my default setting, and that comes as such a relief. I take the mind of Christ for me today. I'm going to stay here awhile and tune my ear to You. I need Your wisdom. Help me, Lord.

Even though I recognized that the Holy Spirit was calling me to worship, my mind kept wandering. I wanted clarity for the issues I was facing, but God simply desired my worship, and I could feel the tussle within me. The little worship I did manage to offer was riddled with distracted thoughts.

I went into the day knowing I hadn't really done what I had been called to do. I had come before the Lord, but I had kept my concerns at the forefront, when He had called me to minister to Him instead. It was a lesson the Lord would keep bringing me back to.

Day 40

The City Council had asked me to suggest a photographer who could represent our city at a large upcoming exhibition in Istanbul. This was a fantastic opportunity for one of our foreigners to become more widely known and respected in the industry, but it was also a chance to showcase our city from a rarely-seen perspective. We had several talented and passionate photographers in our working group, but in my spirit, I felt strongly that our American friend, who had lived in Bursa for nearly a decade, was the man for this occasion.

Kerry was a professional photographer who, along with being a great help in our working group, had focused his expertise on one small but significant village on the outskirts of our city. Kerry had visited this village every week for several years, eventually earning the respect of the elders, and had been given the rare privilege of capturing traditional village life through the lens of his camera. With his gentle manner and technical ability, Kerry had compiled a wonderful array of photographs—a bridge of sorts between vastly different cultures.

Lord, I've always had a clear sense of what is best in a situation. I trust my intuition, and it doesn't often let me down. But Father, there's something more to this. It's as if *You* want Kerry to be honored at that exhibition. It feels weighty, Lord, like I couldn't bear it if he turned down the opportunity. I feel how much You want him there, how proud You are of this man.

Lord, I don't know why this feels so important. It's like You've taken me beyond intuition, beyond exhortation, and now You've drawn out something prophetic in me, and everything in me *longs* for Kerry to embrace this offer. He's so gifted, so qualified, so unbelievably good at what he does. But God, he's also one of the humblest, most under-the-radar people I know; he would never want to take advantage of the people in the village, and he's certainly not chasing fame.

I don't know why, but I actually feel scared. I feel like this is so important. . . and what if he doesn't go for it? It seems presumptuous to speak into someone else's life like this.

There was more to my hesitation, too. While I could easily lead a mixed group of men and women at the city council, the opposite was true when it came to anything vaguely spiritual.

Now this thought, which was obviously from God, messed with my mind, and to be honest, I was scared. Was God giving me, a woman, an idea from Him, to pass on to a man I deeply respected? The whole thing felt very presumptuous.

Anya, take heart from this: I am the Hero of this story—you simply belong to Me. It's not about you.

Thank You, Lord. But I feel so strongly about this. It's hard to let go of.

That's because my Spirit is within you, and I too feel strongly about it. I love Kerry, and I love this city. Be passionate about this, but don't make it about you, dear.

Would you give me something from Your Word for this situation? I'd love a story about a woman who gave a message to a man, who then. . .

I have something for you, and no, it's not about women or men. In my kingdom, being male or female is not a hinderance. In Christ, it doesn't matter. Look in Exodus.

Wow. That was easy. You gave me a story about artists!

Yes. Read what Moses said to the people.

ALL WHO ARE GIFTED ARTISANS AMONG YOU SHALL COME AND MAKE ALL THAT THE LORD HAS COMMANDED . . .
EXODUS 35:10

Well Lord, there's no doubt Kerry is gifted. He's a real artist, and I know he loves You. So why do I feel so hesitant to write to him about this?

You prayed: 'it is all about You, God, and not about me,' but then you forgot that I play the main part. Read on . . .

EXODUS 36:2
'THEN MOSES CALLED . . . EVERY ARTISAN WHOSE HEART WAS STIRRED.'

It struck me that Moses didn't feature much. He just put out the call for artists. But the people were already willing, and God had already stirred their hearts.

EXODUS 35:21-22
'THEN EVERYONE CAME WHOSE HEART WAS STIRRED AND EVERYONE WHOSE SPIRIT WAS WILLING. THEY CAME, AS MANY AS HAD A WILLING HEART.'

So Lord, I figure I can write to Kerry and just tell him about the invitation, and trust You for the result?

Thank you for listening to Me.

Day 41

Lord, it's done. I was interrupted by one thing after another, and that incredible tiredness came over me again—I could hardly put two words together—and now I realize it was all designed to keep me from simply typing an email and getting it sent. I hope we're not too late.

> *But you trusted Jeff when he told you not to fuss. He communicated My thoughts to you exactly when he said, 'the devil is in the delay.'*

Lord, I now stand in Jesus' name and reserve this opportunity for my friend, Kerry. He isn't even in Turkey right now, and I have no idea if he will even be here for the exhibition, but I've done my part, Lord. I've put out the invitation. Please stir his spirit; give him a willing heart. May he be blessed, and may Your name be honored. Lord Jesus, stand and stretch out your arm over that opportunity and set it apart for Kerry, I pray.

Kerry replied a few days later. He would represent our city at the exhibition.

Thank you, Lord.

Day 42

Lord, it's been weeks since I found unhurried and uninterrupted time to fellowship with You. You have been kind to me though. Thank you for refreshing our family each morning as we've gathered in the lounge room and listened to sermons online. You nourish our souls even here, where there's no church to speak of and none of the usual supports. Thank you, Lord Jesus, for being so near to us— and for bringing us close to each other as a family too. I read Psalm 104 this morning and my heart was stirred to agree. *'Bless the Lord, O my soul! Oh Lord my God, you are very great!'*

As I read Psalm 104, another vivid picture of our city came to my mind. The Psalm describes the vibrant interaction between the spiritual world and the natural world. As I read descriptions of hills and mountains, rushing streams and rising waters, it was as if the words described the unseen dynamics that impact and define our city.

Lord, are you giving me a picture of our city of Bursa?

> *Yes, this is for you, dear. I called you to a place absolutely overtaken by jealousy and division. Like a deluge, these evils have flooded the city. It's nearly impossible to rise above the awful tide of jealousy and division here*

in Bursa.

So true, Lord. Jealousy and division wreak havoc here, in government departments, business circles, among neighbors and friends, in schools and the university and expat community; even, I suppose among those who follow You.

> *My people are affected, for sure. They try to rise above it, but we're talking about a province that has been absolutely overtaken.*

Lord, how do I respond?

> *Picture the flood of Noah's time, Anya. Water rose over the face of the whole earth. It tarried so long that nearly everything died. In the end, only a handful of people escaped—but even then, they had to live with the situation that was left behind.*

Your word says that the waters even covered the mountains. That's vivid here, Lord. Mt Uludağ towers above this city. If it was submerged right to its peak, there would certainly be not one part of this entire province spared.

> *Now, see what I did:*

AT MY REBUKE, THEY FLED; AT THE SOUND OF MY THUNDER, THEY TOOK TO FLIGHT.
THE MOUNTAINS ROSE, THE VALLEYS SANK DOWN TO THE PLACE WHICH I APPOINTED FOR THEM. I SET A BOUNDARY WHICH THEY SHOULD NOT PASS SO THAT THEY MIGHT NOT AGAIN COVER THE EARTH. PSALM 104: 7-9

Lord, I understand You want to rebuke jealousy and division in Bursa. You want these evils to recede—to be removed, so that our city will become all You intended. You want to set a boundary around our province that jealousy and division may not penetrate.

Yes. And I'm calling on you to join me.

Our family had enjoyed a huge level of favor and friendship with the Turkish locals and with the Christians in our city. Everyone was committed to working together, at least in principle. The reality was though, that we were all striving for unity in an environment that seemed predisposed towards strife. It was with a great deal of respect for our friends and for the city we lived in, that I began to take a stand against the forces that sought to divide and weaken us.

In Jesus' name, I rebuke Jealousy and Division in the province of Bursa. I rebuke Jealousy and Division in the government, the municipality, the council, and the surrounding regions. I rebuke their interference in the university and schools, in the foreign and Turkish companies, among neighbors and between individuals.

I rebuke Jealousy and Division in the expat community and for any way they operate among the followers of Jesus. I rebuke jealousy and division in my family and in my own life. In Jesus' name, I command these forces to recede. Look! He has set a boundary around this province, and you may not intrude again. The boundary of this

province is now your boundary too. Never again may you have Bursa or her residents . . .

Anya, just as the waters of Noah's flood took time to recede, so it will be here.

I'm asking you to wait, to be patient, to look for signs of new life. Continue to speak against these destructive elements. Mourn their catastrophic effect. But hope in Me, for I will renew this land.

I glimpse your promise, Lord Jesus.

YOU MAKE SPRINGS GUSH FORTH IN VALLEYS,
FLOWING BETWEEN THE HILLS . . .
GIVING DRINK TO EVERY BEAST. THE BIRDS . . .
HAVE THEIR HABITATION; THEY SING AMONG THE BRANCHES.
FROM YOUR LOFTY ABODE, YOU WATER THE MOUNTAINS;
THE EARTH IS SATISFIED . . .

YOU CAUSE GRASS TO GROW FOR THE CATTLE,
AND PLANTS FOR MAN TO CULTIVATE . . .
FOOD FROM THE EARTH, WINE TO GLADDEN THE HEART,
OIL TO MAKE HIS FACE SHINE;
BREAD TO STRENGTHEN MAN'S HEART . . .
THE ROCKS ARE A REFUGE . . .

MAN GOES FORTH TO HIS WORK . . . THESE ALL LOOK TO YOU
TO GIVE THEM THEIR FOOD IN DUE SEASON . . .

YOU OPEN YOUR HAND . . . WHEN YOU HIDE YOUR FACE THE
PEOPLE ARE DISMAYED; WHEN YOU TAKE AWAY THEIR BREATH,

THEY DIE . . . WHEN YOU SEND FORTH YOUR SPIRIT, THEY ARE CREATED; AND YOU RENEW THE FACE OF THE GROUND . . . PSALM 104:10-30 ESV

So tell me, what do you see?

I see the province renewed, cared for by You, functioning under Your sovereign rule. I see peace, prosperity, safety, provision and people who know it all comes from You, Lord. I see people who work and rest, who are productive and happy, and at ease with one another. Lord, as Jealousy and Division recede, send forth Your Spirit here in Bursa, I pray.

Whatever you ask!

Day 43

Dear Father, can we start over again? I haven't been worshipping You the way you called me to, and I haven't been dwelling in You. I'm feeling unwell, the schedule is still too full and, I'm sorry, Lord—Jeff and I are bickering again. Please speak to me, Lord. Cleanse and renew me. I feel weak and sinful and sad. But I love You. I'm listening.

Did you hear the sermon you listened to this morning?

The part about dominion?

Yes. You've thought about taking back dominion in big ways—a city or organization, for example—but that sermon talked about taking back dominion over your mood, your temper, your relationships . . .

I heard it, but I didn't really *get it*. This listening happens in the middle of breakfast, Lego, toddlers, doorbells, phones . . . maybe I'll get to listen again later today.

You don't need to. I've given you the hint. I'll teach you. And I'll do it

Day 43

quietly, today. Just tune your ear to me as you go through the day. I'm near.

I tried to listen to the Lord as the day progressed, but, as I got busy with one thing after another, I struggled to hear what He wanted to say . . .

Day 44

Lord Jesus, I feel stuck. What will it take for me to move forward?

That morning I had read an article that encouraged believers who wanted to operate more fully in the gifts of the Holy Spirit to simply ask in faith, and then follow it up with worship. It included a prayer written by Jack Hayford. I decided I would use that suggested prayer today.

'Dear Lord Jesus, I thank and praise You for Your great love and faithfulness to me. My heart is filled with joy whenever I think of the great gift of salvation You have given me so freely. And I humbly glorify You, Lord Jesus, for You have forgiven me all my sins and brought me to the Father. Now I come in obedience to Your call. I want to receive the fullness of the Holy Spirit.

I do not come because I am worthy myself, but because You have invited me to come. Because You have washed me from my sins, I thank You that You have made the vessel of my life a worthy one to be filled with the Holy Spirit. I want to be overflowed with Your life,

Your love and Your power, Lord Jesus. I want to show forth Your grace, Your words, Your goodness and Your gifts to everyone I can. And so, with simple, childlike faith, I ask You, Lord, to fill me with the Holy Spirit. I open myself to You to receive all of Yourself in me.

I love You, Lord, and I lift my voice to praise You. I welcome Your might and Your miracles to be manifested in me, for Your glory and unto Your praise.'

Then I began praising God. I used verses and songs and spoke out my own testimony of His greatness and love in my life. I didn't experience anything unusual or spectacular in that moment, but it a prayer that started out being all about me ended up in a time that was about Him, and that alone made me feel incredibly happy.

Day 45

A few things happened after that. Jeff began livestreaming worship music through the house as we all went to sleep at night. We'd all been sleeping better for it, and were waking refreshed and encouraged.

Jeff and I also decided to safeguard the healing God had brought to our marriage by taking communion together every night before we went to bed. We didn't make a fuss of it at all—we simply thanked Jesus for his death and took bread and wine together in an act of declaration to the unseen realm that we were one in Christ, that all our sins were covered, and that any attack against us had already been annulled by Jesus' sacrifice. Somehow, that simple act, repeated over a few nights, brought fresh momentum to our journey . . .

At the same time, the Lord showed a couple of issues that we had not yet identified. Both were generational, and both were affecting us as a couple. I loved how Jeff was ready and able to deal with them on behalf of us both, and that we could enjoy the victories together.

We both sensed the season was changing in our lives.

Day 46

I read that prayer again this morning, '*My dear Lord Jesus, I come to You now . . .*' and as I prayed it, I really felt like it's time to move on. It's time to come before You in a new way—maybe with new words, or my own words, or maybe with no words at all.

> *Yes! I called you to worship and I want to lead you there. I don't want your reliance on this prayer to hold us back. Look at the words that really meant something more to you this morning.*

'*Holy Spirit, I sincerely receive You as my Counsellor, I honor You as my Lord, I fully open my life to you in every dimension and aspect . . .*'

> *Yes. As you prayed today, these were the words I affirmed. My Spirit rejoiced with yours at those words. So let's move forward together. It's time to become un-stuck.*

Now this is vague to me. Please tell me what you're thinking.

> *Until now, every time you have come before me, you have been the first to speak.*

You have taken the lead, in a way. That has made me glad, much as it makes you glad when your children come to you, chatting away and waiting for your response.

But for us to go deeper in worship, I need to lead you. I want you to come, sit in my presence, and wait for my Spirit to stir. Let me initiate for a while. Then, in turn, your spirit will respond. This is going to delight us both.

Day 47

I WILL CLIMB UP INTO MY WATCHTOWER NOW AND WAIT
TO SEE WHAT THE LORD WILL SAY TO ME AND HOW HE
WILL ANSWER MY COMPLAINT. HABAKKUK 2:1 NLT

HE LIFTS THE POOR FROM THE DIRT AND THE READY FROM
THE GARBAGE DUMP. HE SETS THEM AMONG PRINCES EVEN
THE PRINCES OF HIS OWN PEOPLE! PSALM 113:7-8 NLT

Lord Jesus, I have already been shown such great favor
here in Bursa and now *this*? I can hardly believe it. Working
alongside the leaders of our city felt honor enough, but
these women You've given me the opportunity to speak to?
I sense how incredible they are, every one of them.

It came up in a conversation with a few girlfriends—the idea of
hosting a little day-retreat for the Christian women in our city. We
estimated that there were perhaps forty women in our city of four
million who loved and served Jesus, including those of us who had
come from other countries, and as far as we knew, there had never
been an occasion for them all to come together.

Our excitement grew as we realized what potential such a day held. Most of these women had very little day-to-day connection with each other, and a gathering like this could really bolster our unity and friendship. But more than that, we sensed God's desire to minister fresh encouragement to us all. Living in Turkey came with unrelenting pressures, and the combination of being foreign, Christian and female all at once, seemed to attract endless suspicion, speculation and even, at times, hostility.

An older lady took charge. We could meet in her apartment, she suggested. And to keep it simple, we'd all bring food and have an indoor picnic for lunch. There would be no singing or music—that would certainly bother the neighbors—but . . . and then she looked at me. *'What if you shared the Daughter of Zion story?'*

In her pragmatic mind, the day was sorted. *Venue, food, get the word out, and now we have a speaker.* Perfect. Of course, I agreed. This was exactly what I had prepared those talks for, and the chance to share it with these tender yet faithful women, in one of the most conservative cities in Turkey, was an honor I could barely have imagined.

But on the way home, a troubling question filled my mind.

Lord, Am I ready for this?

Yes! But there is another incident from your past that I need you to revisit.

And then, a short but painful memory re-emerged. I was twenty years old at the time, and had travelled across the world to be with my family in Canada for Christmas. University exams were done, and I was excited to be back in the familiar little town of Three Hills.

It was one afternoon that my mum and I decided to walk to the local supermarket to pick up some groceries. The snow was thick on the ground, the sidewalks were icy, but the Christmas lights that decorated the houses along the street were wonderful. I reached out to link arms with my mum, partly to steady myself, but mostly, I realize now, because all I wanted was to identify with my mum and take my place as a woman beside her.

> *Anya, the Scriptures are full of expressions like, 'When the fullness of time had come,' and 'at the right time.' Those words tell you something about me. Timing is important. That was your moment, there in Canada. My Spirit agreed with your spirit. You were craving affirmation as a woman and you didn't get it. I'm sorry it hurt so much.*

Oh Lord, I long to be affirmed as a woman. Here I am, thirty-eight years of age, married, with four off-the-scale wonderful children, living in Turkey, leading the working group here, teaching, editing, writing, managing people and projects. I'm loving and nurturing and giving hospitality. . . living what appears to be a full life in an adult would. But deep down, I don't feel like I'm up for the task of being an adult. So many of my responses, my fears, my insecurities— are very childlike. Childish, in fact. *I don't know when I became a woman.*

I had girlfriends who, at my high school graduation, held themselves with poise and confidence. Their maturity and self-assurance were evident. I, on the other hand, felt self-conscious and awkward, uncomfortable with being dressed up. Uncomfortable with being me. Now, twenty years later, I still felt like a perpetual teenager, playing the role of an adult, and hoping it was convincing.

In my daydreams it was different. I could play the piano with confidence and abandon, I stood before crowds and delivered stirring speeches, I could literally walk into any situation and change the world.

Lord, I love that in a few weeks I will have the opportunity to speak to a room full of women. I have the message ready, and I know You will help me. But I sense that it is very important that we address this topic first. I don't want to feel like I'm a girl pretending to be all grown up. I want to know deep within me that I am a woman speaking to her peers. I want to be affirmed.

Remember Eve.

Thank you, Lord. Eve had no other woman to affirm her. But Eve shared the very essence of Adam. She was named in relation to him. Her identity was firmly connected to her oneness with him, *just as I find my identity in Christ!*

Yes! You are in Christ, and Christ is in God.

So, dear God. I'm listening for Your word. I strain to hear Your voice calling forth the woman in me—the woman I am. The woman I am in You.

Lord Jesus, You bring all things to maturity. When You begin a good work, You complete it. I declare that I am in Christ, treasured, whole, mature, complete in Him.

Pause a moment, Anya. Lift up your eyes.

I see mountains outside the window, Lord. I want to be settled in my heart about this, established, like those mountains.

I'm going to answer this need of yours from the Daughter of Zion talks you have prepared. Read the story quietly, Anya. Let my Spirit speak with yours. Do you see?

Yes. At the start, the Daughter of Zion comes across as a confident woman, yet she is immature. She's presumptuous. I have spent a lot of time studying her wounds and shame, but now I see her immaturity.

What does that look like? How is she described before the story turns and she is welcomed home?

Well, she is threatened but she's blasé, she's complacent, comfortable, cared-for, but she gets tossed around by her circumstances. She's quickly cast down and emotionally fragile. I guess she's also prone to despair and loneliness and being misunderstood; she's susceptible to bondage; she's restless, self-conscious, open to criticism and accusations and she has a shortsighted view of the future.

Yes. And then Jesus comes into the story. But I want you to see something. Jesus did not take human form only to identify with her and to share her humanity. The point of his coming was to rend the veil so that she could share His glory.

*Anya, being a woman is more about **where** you dwell. Outside the veil* *is a great, restless multitude. It's possible to grow old out there, but never mature in the most inner place. Everything out there is a poor replica of what it could be. Even the women. The women who are truly whole and restored are those who dwell with me.*

The Daughter of Zion is living in eternity. She's living in the Spirit, she is joyful and content, confident and worshipful. When she speaks, her voice is strong, she 'shouts joyfully to Me!' A woman in my heavenly home is not self-conscious—she's transformed! She's dead to self and alive to Christ. In my presence, she's healed, dignified, blessed and validated because she's seated with Christ.

Do you see? You wanted to walk beside your mum and find validation. But in the heavenlies, you walk with Christ. You are one with Him. There is no doubt about your maturity when you walk with Me.

Lord Jesus, I come once again to that great river with its supply of forgiveness that never runs dry, and I walk into that healing stream. I allow it to wash over that scene in Canada twenty years ago. Lord Jesus, please forgive me for every bitter, broken response I have had because of what took place that day.

Anya,

JERUSALEM ABOVE IS FREE—AND SHE IS OUR MOTHER. GALATIANS 4:26 NIV

Lord, I declare that I am not only my mother's daughter and I am not stuck in some sort of maturity-limbo. In Your realm, I am the daughter

of a glorious City. My head is high, my voice strong, my heart free, my soul secure, and my spirit healed.

Lord, in your presence, nothing can separate me from Your love; in the heavenlies, I am dressed in splendor. My face shines with Your glory. My bones are strong, and my steps are sure. Here I feast on your abundance and drink from your river of joy.

I declare that my identity does not derive from the world, nor from any other person, however dear. I am in Christ, and He calls me His own. My mother could have told me I was a woman, but I suspect that even she could not have convinced me. I am complete only because of You, Jesus. I am elevated to where You are. I can freely approach Your throne. I can commune with You. I can perceive Your desires. *This* is womanhood. This is maturity.

Anya, whatever is holding you back from enjoying my presence—cast it aside. The hours on earth fly by. Dwell with me now, even while you live on earth. Lay aside the hindrance and distractions and be my woman.

Day 48

Oh God. Liberty is asleep. The candle is lit, coffee is poured and my new Bible is open. In twenty minutes, two more children will be dropped off at our place. Can we do this, Father? Can we commune deeply in this tiny window of time?

That afternoon, I began reading in John chapter 1. When I got to verse 38, I paused. 'JESUS SAW THOSE WHO FOLLOWED HIM AND ASKED, '*WHAT ARE YOU SEEKING?*'

It was as if he had asked the question of me directly. I thought awhile. We had spent two solid years in Turkey and right now, what I was seeking was a rest. I was looking for some soul-nourishment, some inspiration, maybe some fresh sights and sounds . . .

Jesus' followers answered the question with a longing of their own. 'LORD, WHERE ARE YOU STAYING?'

Right then, I identified completely with those followers, despite the centuries between us.

Lord, I'm seeking Your Home. I want to find a place outside this world. I come looking for Zion. Oh Lord, will you take me there?

Anya, I say to you what I said to them: 'Come and see.'

SO THEY CAME AND SAW . .
AND STAYED WITH HIM THAT DAY. JOHN 1:39 ESV

Father, I long to come and stay awhile with You.

Day 49

After a particularly draining few weeks, we had taken a short break in Cyprus where we stayed with a family who led a 24/7 Prayer Room. As I took time out with God in their home, I felt God nudge me about pessimism, something I had always figured was just part of who I was—my personality.

> *Anya, I love that your wounds have been healed and the strongholds in your life are dealt with—You are whole and you are free. But I also want to restore your personality. For the calling on your life, there must also be integrity. The negativity and pessimism need to go.*

Thank you so much, Lord. I repent of my constant negativity and ask Your forgiveness. My glass always feels half empty while Jeff's is always half full, and I have become a drain to live with. I'm sorry for always complaining and criticizing and feeling hard-done-by. I know it's not justified.

DO EVERYTHING WITHOUT COMPLAINING OR ARGUING. PHILIPPIANS 2:14 NLT

I call my soul to a new default setting—to overflow with thankfulness, to abound in hope. Oh my soul, do everything without complaining and arguing. I call you to a bright outlook on life.

Lord Jesus, You are so very kind. You've opened my eyes to see the beauty of Your people who have loved us, served us, and blessed us. Thank you for the use of a car so that we can explore this island and find the space we crave. Thank you for the new friend who generously offered to take us all sailing for Eric's birthday this week. Thank you for the clothes and shoes that have been passed on to our kids right when they needed them.

> *That's good, Anya. Thankfulness becomes you. Now one more issue, and this is about being a clean vessel, fit for service. We need to talk about your language. When you are angry or overwhelmed, I hear slang and swearing and unhelpful fillers that lack dignity. It greatly displeases me, Anya. Those words offend me.*

WHAT YOU SAY FLOWS FROM WHAT IS IN YOUR HEART. LUKE 6:45 NLT

I took a piece of paper and listed all the words I have got into the habit of saying in my worst moments, and then, as a display to the spiritual realm that I was rejecting and discarding those words from my vocabulary, I tore them up and then, one by one, I threw them away.

Lord, I come to uproot this language from the soil of my life. I repent of using Your name in vain and in despair and exasperation. Your name, Lord, is a strong tower. Please forgive me for being so offensive and for allowing this offense to come between You and me. I also ask Your forgiveness for the careless words I have been in the habit of speaking. Even when Jesus was dying, he spoke words full of grace. I take my place in Him once again.

Dear Spirit of God, please touch my lips and purge me from sin. Teach me to speak words from heaven. Grant me a renewed, larger, more rich vocabulary. I long to replace this base language with something more beautiful than I've known before. Dear Spirit of God, would You fill my lips with praise? With words that honor Christ and exalt the precious Father? Let grace and dignity and beauty that surpasses earth's norms, be mine in language, I pray.

For You, Lord, for You. Xo

Day 50

Father, I woke up last night with a sense that You were calling me to be an Intercessor. Now that You've done so much for Jeff and me, I long to pray effectively for others in their relationships too. Jesus, you are a constant intercessor, and so is the Holy Spirit. What an amazing thing to partner with You for people and their situations. But to join You, Holy Spirit, I need to speak Your language—I want to come before the Father with words and phrases and utterances that agree with His desires and heart. . .

Day 52

THEY SHALL BUILD UP THE ANCIENT RUINS; THEY SHALL RAISE
UP THE FORMER DEVASTATIONS; THEY SHALL REPAIR THE RUINED
CITIES, THE DEVASTATIONS OF MANY GENERATIONS.

THE SPIRIT OF THE LORD GOD IS UPON ME, BECAUSE THE LORD
HAS ANOINTED ME TO BRING GOOD NEWS TO THE POOR: TO
BIND UP THE BROKENHEARTED, TO PROCLAIM LIBERTY TO THE
CAPTIVES, AND THE OPENING OF THE PRISON TO THOSE WHO
ARE BOUND; TO PROCLAIM THE YEAR OF THE LORD'S FAVOR . . .
ISAIAH 61:1-4 ESV

Lord, thank you for showing me these verses in a new way
today. I always thought the Gospel was all about getting our
sins forgiven and then basically holding on until, one day up
ahead, when we all get to heaven, everything will be made
right.

But these verses say something quite different. The thing
that's really good news for humanity is this: broken hearts get
to be healed, captives find freedom, and right now, in this life,
we all get to live under the favor of God.

Day 53

Our family had spent the week packing again, cleaning our house in Bursa, and saying goodbye to the many friends we had come to love. It was time to move on. For the next year we were going to live in the Mediterranean province of Antalya, and though we didn't know it yet, much of that year would be spent alongside other people as they too confronted the brokenness, bondage and confusion in their lives.

But for now we were in Cyprus, and this particular night we had been invited to join our hosts in the prayer room. I had an inkling of what prayer rooms are like—we had often livestreamed worship and prayer from IHOP in Kansas City, and I had devoured Pete Greig's book, *Red Moon Rising* in one riveting sitting. The prayer room we visited in Cyprus had the same feel. About ten other people came that night; one played quiet worship music on a small keyboard, every now and then interspersing the notes with readings from Psalms or Song of Songs, others stood in silent prayer, some journaled or sketched as they drew near to God. People were free to come and go as they pleased throughout the night, but for now, we settled in for an unbroken time of worship and intercession and basking in the presence of God.

Somehow, in that space, there came a moment for me when it was as if heaven and earth were united—I couldn't pinpoint whether I was or here or there—and as I silently prayed and worshipped, I found myself in the middle of a vivid and profound scene.

In my vision, I was standing, hidden out of sight, clutching the folds of the great curtain that was torn when Jesus died on the cross. As I peeked through to the other side, I found myself looking into the throne room of heaven. I began to write . . .

Larnaca 24/7 Prayer Room

I peer into the throne room.
I don't want to be seen or heard.

HIS EYES SEEK THOSE WHOSE HEARTS ARE TRULY HIS.

You, Lord, see me. You are looking for a bride, and you have seen *me*. . .

I'm hearing voices from the past, '*Children should be seen and not heard*,' but I don't want to be seen *or* heard. I'm just looking. . .

'*I hear you, Anya. I hear your voice, your heart. But I want to **see** you.*'

Lord, I don't want to be seen. Maybe if I looked well and lovely. But not now. Not here.

Then I nearly froze. The man we were staying with had stood up, and from across the room, he was coming toward me. He stopped and picked up a piece of satiny red fabric from a basket by the wall, came and stood directly in front of me, and with a few quiet words about fire falling on me from heaven, he draped it over my head.

No one else in the room seemed to notice or care—they were all absorbed in their own interactions with God, but I was mortified. Not only did I not want to be singled out in my vision, but I certainly did not want to be singled out here in this room full of people. I didn't want to be rude, but as soon as I could, I let the fabric fall to my shoulders.

Oh God, why did he do that? And why did he tell me it's a symbol that the fire will fall on me? I don't like that thought at all. Those words do nothing but annoy me and distract me. It's a small enough room and I feel self-conscious already in this unfamiliar environment, Lord. I desperately do not want to stand out and look stupid, and now I am draped in ridiculous red satin. It's been a long time since I felt this embarrassed.

> *Anya—step inside a minute. You're hiding, even from Me. I want to tell you something. I am looking, and I see you. Not because I want to make you squirm under my gaze, but because I'm looking for a Queen—a bride. That red fabric? It is a royal robe. Take my hand. I want to lead you up to a throne.*

Lord, this is a wedding! Who is it for? Who are You? Who am I being united with? Who am I to be bride to? Who am I being seated with?

Not with me, Anya. With my Son. I am the Father. My Son is on the throne, and I want you to take your place in royalty, seated next to Him.

Right then, I asked the Father a strange question.

Is this a marriage of convenience?

No, my daughter. This is an arranged marriage.
I looked, I saw you, and I chose you to be the bride of my Son. Out of many, I chose you!

Oh Lord. So this is what *Father* means. You chose me for Your one and only, beloved Son? You chose *me* to rule and reign with him? To bring him glory?

Yes! Exactly . . . now come, let us walk this aisle together. Only heavenly eyes will see you. Walk in dignity and splendor and simplicity. Take the hand of my beloved Son. You are his! Sit, my chosen daughter, at his side.

Now listen! The angels are rejoicing. They are praising Him, your husband, your Lord, your bridegroom. They see you and share your joy, but it's Him they praise and worship. See how you are not the focus? Not the object of their gaze? Your union with Him, your reigning with Him, only increases their love and admiration of the Man you also love.

So, Anya, you can join them! You too can worship and treasure Him. Your voice is precious to Him, and to me. Let your heart swell with pride and affection for my Son.

You and I share this unspeakable love of Him. Now—is this too much for you? You've hidden in the background for so long.

Dear Father—His Father and mine! No, this feels fine. Somehow perfectly natural, like I was born for this. I feel like Mary, the girl from Tasmania, who become Queen of Denmark—or Kate Middleton, marrying the future King of England. This is a fairytale. A girl's dream come true. My heart's desire.

But even those princesses were not chosen by their husband's father! It honors me beyond words that You chose me for Your Son. I know You and He are One. Nothing could be more perfect.

Day 54

So many times, Father, I have prayed the words of that prayer, *'anoint me for all of my life and walk and calling.'* I want to ask You, am I anointed?

> *Anya, you know you are set apart. But today, I want to anoint you afresh for the calling on your life.*

Lord, I come and receive your anointing. As You pour out Your anointing oil over me, it drenches my head, runs down over my shoulders and Lord, I accept this lavish anointing upon every part of my life. May this truly be the 'oil of joy' for me—the joy that eluded me for so many years. Thank you, my God.

That night . . .

> *Anya, tonight when you were out, a lady who only met you for a few minutes asked Jeff to pass on the message that you are 'a Deborah'. Do you recall your prayer this morning?*

Oh yes! You anointed me for my calling, and I accepted it—and I asked you to confirm it to me through someone else today.

Read the story of Deborah. Go to Judges 4 and 5.

Oh Father! She spoke for You. She led Your people from oppression to freedom, from bondage into victory. She prophesied. She led the way into battle. She declared the strong man *beaten.* And because of her ministry, other women were empowered to bring down the enemy.

> *Yes! You too will lead women to spiritual victory. Mothers delivering families, and so much more. Time and time again, people will know that Satan has again been silenced by the words of a woman; rendered powerless by her hand. And at the end of it all, there's a song! A happy song of praise, a testament to all I have done.*

Lord, I acknowledge this 'Deborah spirit.' I bless all the women who shall rise because of my influence. And I bless every man who shall accompany me in this calling.

YOU ANOINT MY HEAD WITH OIL. MY CUP OVERFLOWS.
PSALM 23:5 NIV

This morning I received your anointing, Father and already there is overflow. Wondrous God! I love you.

Day 55

Dear Father, while we're speaking of joy, did you see me sprawled on my bed as a teenager in Australia, looking up every scripture reference to joy and happiness? I just wanted to figure out how to be happy.

I know. Do you want to know where I was at the time?

Of course. And I would like to know why I never found the joy I was longing for, Father. Why didn't You fill me?

Anya, happiness has not been a strong trait in your family, has it? Something started this absence of joy, and it's never been forgiven.

So, did this begin well before my time?

Yes. You're right.

I don't even know if it's important, but how many generations has it been? And how did joylessness get the right to invade us?

It's a melancholy spirit, Anya. I put the desire in your family to work as artists, but they rarely had the chance to live out their calling. You have a heritage of people who worked hard and had good jobs, but there was not as much joy in their work as I intended.

And here I am, about to start the work of a lifetime—and I long to do it with joy.

Then start by forgiving.

Lord, I speak forgiveness over the generations— those who came before me whose lives displayed so little joy. I lavishly apply Your forgiveness and mine across the generations, and trust You to realign our work that we might find joy in what we do.

Forgive me too, Lord, for being a joyless wife and mother, and for all the sin which stems from joylessness—despair, faithless words, negativity, morbid thoughts. . .

Thank you, Lord Jesus, for bearing all my sorrow away. I long to dwell in Zion, in Your presence, where there is fullness of joy and pleasures forevermore.

Except, Lord, I've become horribly sarcastic lately too.

I know, dear, and it grieves my spirit. Sarcasm and dry humor are good for masking misery when the joy of life is absent.

Lord, what is the root of this joylessness?

The Lord brought to my mind the freemasons—a society that my grandfather had been a member of. Freemasonry was a strong component of New Zealand life in his generation and was best known for its secrecy.

> *Anya, there have been many secrets in your family. People put on a veneer of a smile, but even you could see how fake it was. No one smiled from their spirit.*

Oh Lord, such brokenness. Such captivity. Please bind us up. Forgive my family, forgive us all. Forgive the sin and secrecy and deception. In the name of the Lord Jesus I release Your forgiveness over us all. Forgive me, God, especially, for the sarcasm that has pervaded my speech. I speak forgiveness over all the generations, washing every joyless life with Your forgiveness. Have mercy on us, Lord.

> *Anya, your sin is cleaned. Your iniquity is taken away. Now fight for your children.*

In the powerful name of Jesus, I declare the spirits of joylessness and melancholy have no legal right to my life, or my children's lives. I command you to release any hold you have on my children. I free the artistic spirit in them. In Christ, beauty and inspiration and originality and creativity are boundless. Sadness, joylessness, melancholy—I now cast you off. I renounce your right to my life and to my family line for the generations to come.

You must never return. All is forgiven.

I worship you, Father, my deliverance, my rock, my healer. Praise You for your victory . . .

Anya, now seal off this deliverance and seek filling with joy.

Father, please pour out Your Spirit upon me. The fruit of the Spirit is pure joy. I seek You, I seek Your presence, Lord. There is an ocean of joy for me—wave after wave, breaking over me. Lord, let nothing ever rob me of this joy. Please change my temperament. Transform my personality. Bring me to health and wholeness. Let me rejoice and be glad.

PART FOUR

By this stage, I knew that the spiritual and emotional clutter that had accumulated across my lifetime was largely cleared away. Now just one thing surfaced: I still had an orphan-spirit. Once that was dealt with, the devil would have to completely loose his hold on me. I was about to embark on an incredible week . . .

Day 56

Dear Lord, I love how you've got Jeff and I on this journey to wholeness and sanctification. Thank you for showing such a personal interest in us. But for a few days You have been highlighting this subject of the 'orphan spirit' to me. I'm keen to know what this is about.

We found a few sermons online and God, I thank you for the way they laid out such a strong Biblical perspective. I never thought of You creating Adam as Your son—that his first and only understanding was that You were his Father, walking with him, talking, handing over authority, delighting in him, meeting his needs. I saw how Satan's point of entry was to take away his sense of sonship. No wonder You made such a plan to rescue and retrieve Your children. Thank you, Lord.

I also learned how the disciples were taught to pray *'Our Father, who is in heaven . . . Your Kingdom come.'* I love that we belong to a Kingdom that has, at its head, a *Father*. Kingdom and family are entwined.

But what do we do with all this Lord? The whole planet has been orphaned from You, and even as your child, I realize I am prone to living like an orphan. I call You Father, but I have so little sense of Your Fatherhood in my life.

Let's start by talking about orphans.

I made a long list of orphan-traits. I was surprised by how many there were, and how they seemed to touch on every area of life. From aloneness to living in survival mode, to having no real grasp of their preciousness . . . the list went on for pages. I knew I was onto something. The Lord was highlighting the ways an orphan-spirit was evident in my life. Then, He capped it all off with an astoundingly simple revelation.

Anya, even orphans have their own unique story. But let me tell you the one sure identifier of all orphans.

What's that?

They have no daddy. Some have been adopted and have learnt to call out 'father,' or even, 'dad.' But, 'Daddy?' Never. Usually they just leave off any term that identifies them as a child of anyone. If orphan babies cry out for their daddy, he doesn't come. Even if someone cares for them, it's still not their daddy. There is no one who can take a daddy's place. Before long, it just sounds baby-ish to even use the name.

I felt a combination of fear and apathy take hold of me. This idea of an orphan spirit seemed to touch on some deep places in my life, and yet I sensed that if I did not face this topic, I would never fully reach spiritual maturity.

HOW LONG WILL YOU SIMPLE ONES LOVE YOUR SIMPLE WAYS? IF YOU HAD RESPONDED TO MY REBUKE I WOULD HAVE POURED OUT MY HEART TO YOU AND MADE MY THOUGHTS KNOWN TO YOU. PROVERBS 1:22-23 NIV

Dear Father, I repent of my clinging to ignorant, simplistic living whilst You have been inviting and drawing me into spiritual maturity. God, more than anything, I desire to know Your poured-out heart and thoughts.

BUT WHOEVER LISTENS TO ME WILL LIVE IN SAFETY, AND BE AT EASE, WITHOUT FEAR OF HARM. PROVERBS 7:33 NIV

Dear Savior, though I have tottered on the threshold and taken many looks back over my shoulder at my life thus far . . . Lord, I turn to embrace the future. This is not my time for returning down paths I have already explored. Please be gracious to me. Fill me with boldness beyond myself. Help me, dear God, to abandon myself to You. I am the prodigal son. I'm returning, and I want to hear Your rebuke.

There is no rebuke for you, Anya. Just a robe and a ring and my love.

God, really? All I long for is for You to pour out Your heart and thoughts to me. Tell me fresh things, Lord. I don't want to read more about you right now. I want to *commune* with You. This is intimacy. I'm terrified, but I crave it. I crave You.

BUT WHOEVER LISTENS TO ME WILL LIVE IN SAFETY . . .

I pray that verse, Lord. Orphans are not safe, but sons and daughters are. Thank you, Lord. I fear a dangerous life. It's not noble or exciting to me anymore. I want to walk assured of safety. I turn my ear, waken my ear, to hear Your voice.

. . . AND BE AT EASE.

Oh God, I long for this—to be completely at ease in my soul. No more anguish and longing and restlessness. As I listen and receive Your words, Father, bring my spirit to a quiet place, I pray. I come to be set, inwardly, at ease.

. . . WITHOUT FEAR OF HARM.

Father, from this perspective, a life of just listening and responding feels unpredictable, unusual—like all the old cushions will be discarded. But not only do I believe You will do me no harm—Lord, you will even remove the *fear* of harm. For that, I very deeply praise You.

Now Lord, I come to make this great exchange. I give You all my fear, and I take from You, dear God, a spirit of faith. Abundant faith. Strong faith. Faith that speaks to the world, and the world responds. Faith that speaks to the sick, the guilty, the wounded, the lonely, the sad—faith that speaks to wars and conflicts and destruction and burdens. I take from You, Lord, faith that speaks.

Now let's make another great exchange. I want you to cast off the spirit of an orphan and take from me the spirit of sonship, of adoption—this is the spirit that enables you to speak the most faith-filled words of all: 'Abba! Father!'

You welcome my Spirit's voice every day. You love Jesus, and you are united with Him, my beloved Son. Now I long for you to stop avoiding me as your Father. You will not be uncomfortable or lost for conversation in my presence any longer.

'Whoever listens to me will be at ease.' Really. But I can't convince you like this. You need to be rid of that orphan heart. I don't want to clean all this up, Anya. There's no need to trawl through all the ways and times and situations that have left you feeling fatherless. Just know that I know, I always knew, that my children would be orphaned, and that I have come to be a father to the fatherless, and now, a father to you.

I was picking up on theological themes I had never known about before, and now, on the brink of an incredible shift in my relationship with God, one of my greatest fears came to the surface.

Lord, I'm scared that all these steps I'm taking will alienate me from my friends who haven't walked this path—good, godly men and women who love You, who just faithfully read Your word and pray and serve You. Lord, all of this would, I presume, sound very foreign to them. I hate the thought of being *more* different than we already are.

My dear Anya. This kingdom you have all come into is a family. It's a Kingdom with a Father. The closer you come to me, the more you will be united with your brothers and sisters. I have so many precious children. Let me love on you, Anya, and see how much more you will come to know the love I shed among my children. I will never come between you and your brothers and sisters.

My longing is that you may be one, as we are one. This glorifies me. Don't listen to the lie of the enemy. He divides. I unite. Trust my love in this, Anya.

Okay, Lord, I'm ready. Spirit of God, you are *holy*. Nothing broken or rebellious is in You. This orphan spirit is completely contrary to Your Father-heart. It's in opposition to Your desire to welcome and embrace and bring peace and safety and belonging to me. I've been carrying this orphan-spirit for so very many years. It has closed me off from feeling Your love, the love of my parents, Jeff's love, and the love of others. It's kept me from responding to love and lavishing love on others. I haven't fully received Your love, Father.

Dear one, we will talk soon. But first, we must make another great exchange. You must lay that orphan-spirit down at my feet. This heavy load is no longer for you. Let me relieve you of this orphan spirit. Lay the whole thing down, child.

God, I lay myself at your feet. I give all I am to You. Free me from an orphan-spirit. Thank you. I'm empty. Please fill me. By faith I take from You a new spirit—I take from my smiling Father the spirit of adoption, spirit of sonship, and I say 'Abba, Father! Daddy!' Dearest Father, I am Your child. I belong to You.

But Father, I can't sense Your love.

Daughter, you have only just been restored to me. You have been brought home. I rejoice. But I don't want to overwhelm and scare you. First, I must quiet you with my love. Slowly and naturally I will lead you into revelation of myself. But for just a little while I want to show you that you are safe, that my home is your home, that you're free to be you, that there is plenty here and it's my joy to bestow it on you. I want to watch you become confident, to start asking me for what you want, to watch you become more like me.

Day 57

Father, after giving that orphan-spirit over to You, I felt so much lighter inside. I took Evie out, and we had so much fun together. We laughed and chatted, and I felt like a decent mum for a while.

But Lord, there's one thing that keeps coming up. People keep asking me what I *do*, and I don't know what to say. I can't describe my life. and we don't have the same steady stream of visitors we had in Bursa. We've moved to a new city, and we're not busy here. I feel like I have to *do something, be* something.

Yes. Orphan-spirited people keep busy, because that keeps them from feeling disconnected. Children, on the other hand, don't care for work or busyness. They just want to be with their parents, to dwell together, to be noticed, to play and relax and enjoy the atmosphere of home. That's what I want to give you, Anya. I want you to stop and just be my child. Dwell in my home and let the spirit of worship grow strong in you. Oh, and learn to let your children just dwell as well. They don't always have to be 'pulling their weight.' You should renounce those words and let your kids just be.

You are still young and fragile in your relationship with me, like a shoot that is easily bruised. That's what happened yesterday. You were not receptive to my Father-heart. And you, like a little green shoot, got trampled.

I need watering.

Yes, you do. But remember the promise I gave you. 'He who waters others will himself be watered.' I have made you and Jeff waterers. I will water you. I will refresh you. Just see.

So now, what do I do to recover from yesterday?

You just hide in me. I know what it is to look after a young plant. My beloved Son grew up before Me, his Father, like a young plant (Isaiah 53v2). I know how to care for green shoots. I tend them.

Father, I'm sorry for yesterday. Sorry for all the sin and sadness that I nurtured. Please wash it all away and strengthen my spirit of adoption. I cry out to you, Abba Father, *for You.*

Day 58

Dear Father, this morning I mentioned that the price of gold had dropped, and that it's a good day for buying the little gold coins that are so prevalent here. Then, unexpectedly, just as we were finishing breakfast, Jeff handed me a hundred and fifty lira to go and buy a piece for myself when I went to the mall.

The crazy thing is, I had no idea how to respond. Do I even *want* gold? Do I *really* value it? Maybe I should just keep the money for when we need it. I don't know what to do with this. Father, this feels extravagant and silly. Gold might be the way people here stash away their savings, but it's not like that in the rest of the world. I just want to save a bit for our girls, so we can bless them when they are older. It's not about the gold, exactly.

> *I know, and you are welcome to buy all the gold you can. Just know that I will provide for your children. It's a father's responsibility and pleasure to provide for his children's children. My promise is not only for you but for your children too.*

I will supply all your needs. Your Father knows your needs. Part of living in the spirit of adoption is learning that you will never lack.

Please strengthen my spirit, Father. My dad worked so hard to supply all the needs of a large family and give us a good life.

Yes, that's what Fathers do. Whatever it takes to be sure their children have a home and food and clothing. Only, you don't have to worry about me. I'm your Father in Heaven! I will make sure you are well-supplied.

Thank you, Father. This is still hard for me to believe.

Day 59

I'm swamped by my bad behavior, Collapsed under gunnysacks of guilt . . . Lord, my longing are in plain sight, My groans an old story to you. I'm on the edge of losing it—the pain in my gut keeps burning. I'm ready to tell the story of my failure. I'm no longer smug in my sin . . . Don't dump me, God . . . help me . . . I want some wide-open space in my life. Psalm 38:4,9,17,21-22 MSG

I was so swamped by guilt i couldn't see my way clear. more guilt in my heart than hair on my head . . . I'm a mess. I'm nothing and have nothing. Make something of me. You can do it. You've got what it takes, but God, don't put it off.' Psalm 40:12,17 MSG

Honestly, Lord, getting control over me is like taming a wild horse. What on earth was I thinking, ranting and raving to Jeff like that? It's not that there's lots of conflict any more. But if something unsteadies me, I still take it out on Jeff.

I want to hold onto my healing and never go back to my

old ways, but this morning I blew it. Jeff is always loving and kind and selfless and uses gentle words with me. He is affectionate, and he's real. He's not hiding from me, or keeping himself from me. So why did I explode like that?

I remembered the words a pastor had once shared with us. *'If you want to know what your idols are, look at what makes you angry.'*

God, will you show me my idols?

> *Control, Anya. It's time to smash it down.*

Father, Yes! I was trying to control everything this morning. I can't be free while I cling to control, can I, Lord? The need to control means I have to constantly keep an eye on things, push the right buttons, pull the right strings at the right time. It's exhausting, Lord. But if instead I am controlled by Your Spirit, I'm free to just move as He directs and the pressure is off!

Lord, I stand before this idol of control and smash it to pieces. In Jesus' name, I demolish control in my life. I want to be the one who is *under control*. I place myself today, Lord, under the control of Your Spirit. You alone hold all things together.

> *Now, Anya, just because we're being thorough, and I don't want to leave even a trace of bitterness in you, I want to show you one more thing that came up this morning.*

What is it, Lord?

Jeff wronged you a few times over the years, that's true. But you brought some things up this morning that show that you haven't let it go. You felt pushed around by some of the decisions he made, and you felt under-valued as a wife. He's acknowledged that and its long past, but let's put even the memories to rest. As I bring these instances to your mind, release Jeff into your forgiveness and mine.

Oh Father! Thank you! I release those memories and in Jesus' name I erase them from my mind. I take the place of a cherished wife. I receive Your assurance in my spirit that *I am precious.* Please teach my spirit to dance, to smile and laugh and be free. Teach me joy and pleasure and love, Lord. Please bring this renewed spirit to full maturity in me.

Day 60

Lord, I just realized today that all the tension I have felt toward Jeff all these years is just *gone*. I'm not threatened by him, I'm not feeling critical of him, I'm not ignoring him—in fact, for the first time in our marriage, I'm really listening to him, enjoying him and probably most incredible of all, I feel able to share all that is in my heart. He's getting the real me!

What a change. Father. Thank You. This is a huge deliverance. To think that for all those years, I was so lost. Now I am ready to see what happens when You, God, act to make up for lost time!

Postscript

Months passed and it was Summer again in Turkey when another family came from Australia to visit us. With incredible generosity and an outpouring of their love, they invited us to join them for a week in Cappadocia—a wonderfully unique city that delights tourists from all over the world.

As I sat on the balcony of our hotel one morning and surveyed the valley around me, my mind drifted over all had transpired since the first day I knelt before God on the hand-woven rug in our home in Bursa. I watched Jeff and the children walking up the hill together as the sun's early rays broke through the clouds and expressed my gratitude to god as best I could. . .

Dear Father! Now this feels *and* looks like love! You have wakened joy and delight in me. What a privilege to be Your child. I'm delighting in this crazy mix of Your amazing world, the wonderful people You have created, and *You*! This is a pure gift, Father, this holiday in Cappadocia. I sit here in the early morning—the sun has already warmed the air, the flowers surround me with their vibrant colors and the birds are calling from the branches—to *You*, I'm sure!

I see the gentle donkey by the road, these ridiculously *fun* chimneys made of rock, us sleeping in a *cave*! —the ready smile and joy of the hotelier's family, my children laughing as they ride the velvety horse . . . it's lovely, Lord. Please rummage around my heart and find my deep satisfaction in You and Your kindness today. Thank you so very much for our friends who brought us here with them. Their love for our family is beyond words. Let them *feel* our joy today, and let that be our thanks to them.

Thank you, Father. Is this our inheritance as Your children? If so, it's very, very good, and I delight in You.

Since Then

When I read these journals, I can barely recognize the woman who wrote them. Yes, it's me, but the real me only got to emerge when the pain was gone. I smile when I read it all now because the reality is:

I was broken. Now I'm not.
I was hurting. Now I'm not.
I was powerless. Now I'm not.

I got my God-story!

When people ask me to tell them about my faith journey, I usually begin with, *'Well, I gave my heart to Jesus when I was four years old, but . . .'* and then I go straight to what you have just read in this book, because that's when the burdens I never knew I was carrying, were lifted and I finally *felt* fully alive. In terms of our marriage, our outlook on life, and our experiences of God, the story of this book really has turned out to be, in a very real sense, only the beginning. . .

From Jeff

Jeff, this story comes twelve years into your married life. Obviously while Anya was spending intense time seeking God, you were aware of the bigger picture . . .

Yes, Turkey seemed to come out of left field for our family, but we traced it to a new way of praying. We had started to ask God if we could join Him in what He was doing rather than simply asking Him to come alongside us in our plans. It seemed impossible, the thought of moving a family of six across to the other side of the world. In the end we handed it over to the Lord. If it was His idea, then He would need to pull it off. And He did. Nine months later Anya and I were scouting out cities on the West coast of Turkey as potential destinations for our family.

The journey to Turkey brought out the best in Anya. She was by that time an old hand at cross cultural situations and undaunted by the challenge of the transition. Anya has friends—many more than most of us have! —and they quickly rose in support of our family to formed what we called, our 'Team of Friends.' These incredible people followed our journey and supported us in every possible way for the entire duration of our time in Turkey.

Preparing to leave Australia was challenging. It was a bit of an emotional roller coaster. About this time the Lord quietly started to teach both of us about spiritual realities. The unseen realm became more substantial to us and we started to see we had more spiritual tools available to us than we ever had realized before. God was upskilling us for the daunting pressures that lay ahead.

Both of us would say that Turkey brought out the best and worst in each other. Normal props that we took for granted were no longer there. We needed to dig deep to get through. It was a spiritual wilderness with friends and family and church far away. God went ahead of us and quickly led Anya to get involved with a volunteer foreigner's working group associated with the city council. Two weeks after joining, through a confluence of events, Anya was elected President of the working group. It was a wild ride. That day the Lord suggested she should put her hand up and in the evening, she was voted in! The group at first was very cynical of the city council's motives, but over the next two years Anya led the group, growing its membership until it was about five hundred strong. She was loved and deeply respected by the city officials, and had a significant impact in her role.

It was during this time, when there was every indication that Anya was living completely to her potential with success on every side that she took time out to spend time with God and do something about the heaviness she carried. During Ramadan that year she experienced a great breakthrough spiritually (the subject of this book). Since then, Anya has been able to take what she learned during that time and come alongside others in their own personal quest for healing and freedom.

She has become very capable in leading others through prayer ministry. I remember her leading a prayer ministry team for a women's conference in Turkey. It was an amazing time as God turned up in amazing ways. The ministry team didn't sleep for a couple of days and breakthrough was everywhere! It was the start of a new ministry for us both, in a sense, as we realized that amazing potential of coming alongside others in personal healing prayer.

Anya was obviously very concerned about the state of your marriage while you were in Turkey. How was it from your point of view?

I think most people would agree that us men are a bit slow on the uptake about this kind of thing. I guess I am no exception. Some of what's in the book came as a bit of a shock to me. There's no way I would ever have said, 'Oh she has baggage so it's tough for us in our marriage.'

Turkey was an incredible challenge for us though. Probably the first time I was aware of an issue is when we both found ourselves saying, 'There's a problem *in* our marriage.' We both found ourselves taking each other the wrong way over and over and neither of us felt like we had the other's approval. But I didn't see it as an Anya-issue. I guess I saw it as something that had got between us, something outside both of us but certainly impacting our relationship.

I was confused by it, to be honest, but I put it down to general spiritual opposition. It was a little like we were behind enemy lines, away from church and friends and family, and I was aware at the time of a real need to fight for my family like never before. I guess I did that, but my approach was probably more like putting my head down and pushing through. I'm sure to Anya it felt like I was withdrawn—and in a way, that was the case.

During that Ramadan, how aware were you of what Anya was doing?

I knew Anya was getting up early and that she was taking time out to seek God but for the most part I was unaware of the details. It's difficult to remember exactly but I'm pretty sure that I asked her a few times how she was going with what she was doing. I remember praying for her over that month, but it was some time before Anya shared the whole story with me.

What about your marriage? How did Anya's month of focusing on healing for your marriage change things for you as a couple?

In a way, we both recognized that tension between us had just dissipated. Afterward, Anya was noticeably happier. We did a few things together for a while, like take communion before we went to bed each night, and that seemed to safeguard the healing between us. But mostly it was subtle. I think it takes some time to walk things like this out. The truth was that there was a lot of other things going on at the time. Life in Turkey really slows down in Ramadan but generally we were living life at a pretty hectic pace.

How about you? Did you go through a similar healing process?

The truth is that we both needed some work. What Anya discusses in this book is something we both embraced. I was personally surprised at how much baggage I had, and it took a determined effort over a number of years and real obedience to the Spirit to move it on. I found it an unpleasant process, more like mucking out the stalls than anything. By comparison, I admire the courage and intimacy with God that Anya demonstrated as she moved forward with this.

We were both on a similar path but for the most part our timing was completely out of sync. The awesome thing is with that all behind us there is so little between us now. Misunderstanding and frustration have certainly retreated. I think we have both become a truer reflection of our real selves—and we see each other more clearly.

We both agree that what we did was effective not just for our marriage and for us as individuals, but has set future generations up for a new, more healthy 'normal' than we started out with.

And now? What's it like from a bit further down the track?

We came back from Turkey absolutely transformed as a couple—we are both strong people who are very determined and idealistic. I guess that makes 'happily ever after' more challenging than for some. We have always put God first in our individual lives and that has also been true for us as a married couple. That has been a great foundation but there have been plenty of times when we have relied on stick-ability and faithfulness as the glue to keep us together rather than love, romance and harmony. Now, we are just a lot more lighthearted around each other. It's easy, being together. That's no small thing, when you know the whole story! And the healing and freedom we fought for now gets to be our kids' norm, so we have a definite shared sense of confidence as we invest in future generations.

Breaking Down Spiritual Strong-holds

Please note, this is a brief tool, designed to be used in conjunction with the Holy Spirit's prompting and leading, and therefore serves as a general guide.

A spiritual stronghold, wound or area of bondage, is simply an aspect of our lives from which the enemy can preside and operate. The Gospel, however, allows the work of Christ on the cross to have full effect in our lives, including the breaking down of these strongholds. When a stronghold is demolished, we remove the legal right of the enemy to operate in that area.

To start with, carve out an unhurried block of time. It's helpful to have somewhere to jot down thoughts as you get them, and a Bible. We also recommend having someone else praying alongside you if possible.

1. *Come before the Holy Spirit.* Open your ears to Him alone and forbid any confusing or distracting or lying spirit.

2. *Lay open your life before the Lord.* Ask Him to reveal any areas that are broken. Or tell Him about a particular habit or area of bondage that is bothering you.

3. Ask the Holy Spirit to *identify and name the stronghold.* What is the spiritual root? Listen to Him. Wait, and He will bring a word or a memory to mind so you know what you are deal-

ing with. Then bring it into the light and name it in His presence. 'Lord, I name the stronghold of _____ in my life.'

4. Now come against the stronghold with spiritual weapons:

    a. Word of God

    Declare scriptures against the stronghold, to weaken it. The Holy Spirit can prompt you, or another person or even a concordance may be helpful to point you to relevant verses. Use verses or Biblical events or examples that directly relate to the stronghold and keep going until you sense the stronghold is weakened. E.g. 'I speak this verse against the stronghold of _fear_ in my life: I will trust and not be afraid. I declare that perfect love casts out fear . . .' (Isaiah 12:2; 1 John 4:18)

    b. Forgiveness

    Ask the Holy Spirit to show you how this stronghold first got in, and how it has played out in your life. Bring Christ's forgiveness to every person and situation that He brings to mind. You are essentially washing your history clean. 'Lord, I come into Your presence to take a great measure of Your forgiveness, and I wash it over . . .'

    i)   FORGIVENESS FOR PAST GENERATIONS—after forgiving, it's good to declare, 'I cut off this stronghold at it's root. It has no place in my life or in the generations to come.'

    ii) FORGIVENESS FOR OTHERS—for anyone, any institution, any situation or moment that led to this stronghold entering your life or being strengthened.

    iii) FORGIVENESS FOR YOURSELF—for any way

you have opened the door to the enemy's work in your life, for ungodly responses and sin in this area. 'Lord, I take forgiveness for myself. I bathe in Your forgiveness. . .'

As you proceed, you may recall words that others have spoken over you, or words you have spoken that have given the enemy an open door. Take a moment to renounce and reject those words from your life.

Again, keep going until the Holy Spirit has brought all the memories to mind that He wants you to forgive. You will know deep down when the job is done!

5. Finally, break down the stronghold in your life once and for all. Just as Christ declared His work finished, we do too. 'In the name of the Lord Jesus, I now break down the stronghold of _____ in my life. I tear it down completely, until it is absolutely demolished. I declare the stronghold of _____ destroyed forever in my life, and in the life of my family to a thousand generations.'

Now wait on the Lord. You will either have peace that the job is done, or you might become aware that evil spirits have also had an influence. If that is the case, simply name them, bind them, and command them to go in Jesus' name and present themselves before the Lord, awaiting His command, never to return.

6. In place of the stronghold, invite and declare the word of God. There are blessings and life-giving traits that are yours in Christ. Lay hold of them in His presence. Declare scrip-

tures e.g. Where __*fear*__ has been, I now invite __*cour-*__ __*age.*__ I declare that I am strong and very courageous. I will not be afraid. What can man do to me?!' (Hebrews 13:5-6)

7. Seal off the work. 'Lord, I come to You and ask You to safeguard all the ground I have taken today. Let none of the freedom I have taken hold of today be lost, but rather, may it find full expression in my life and in the life of the generations that follow me. Teach me, Lord, to walk as a free person in this area. In Jesus' name.'

My Thanks

To Jeff. Thank you for believing with me that our story will become a catalyst for breakthrough in the lives of many others. Whatever lies in the past, we've now made up for in record time. Bless you, DH. I love you more than ever.

To Eric, Joseph, Evangeline and Liberty. You have witnessed firsthand this before and after story. Thank you for loving me when I was at my worst. I love your dad more than I can ever put into words and I love, love, love being your mum.

To Diny Adema Endless gratitude for giving me the task of heading up the prayer ministry team at the Antalya Women's Conference. The flow-on effect continues to this day.

. . . and to the Marmaris women. Praying with you was a game-changer for me. I thought I was full of joy after what God had done in my life, but when I saw Him do the same for you, my heart burst and my imagination ran wild. Now I knew there was no stopping the reach of God's healing and freedom. Thank you for sharing your lives with me. Despite the fact we got about three hours sleep all weekend, I came away feeling more alive than ever. I have every one of you in my heart. There truly is no person or place on earth He isn't poised to bless.

To Kerry and Shari, Dave and Ros, Eric and Judith, and Mildred. Without your friendship, our years in Bursa could have made for a lonely story. Instead, we got to share life with some of the best! For living expat lives with such integrity and joy, we honour you.

To Janelle Knox and Ruth Maxwell. You are my women in ministry, my go-to mentors and my with-you-all-the-way friends. Thank you for being encouragers and facilitators over the years and thank you for all you've done to help this book go far and wide.

To Samantha Woodland, Leanne Gehlen and Anne Burrows. You were the first to read my story and your enthusiasm meant the world. For coming back with the most endearing feedback ever, thank you.

To my amazing ARISE Church life group. You have cheered me along the way. Thank you for every prophetic word, for every faith-filled prayer, and most of all, for being so real. You can't imagine how it spurred me on knowing that Tuesday nights were coming.

To Nina and Hannah. For taking my handwritten journals and typing them up, thank you. Thank you for being so receptive to what God had done in me. And to **Basia**. Sitting around my lounge room as a foursome, sharing our lives and dreams and championing each other over endless cups of tea, made for a very happy year.

To Kelly Burgess. Thank you for taking this book and designing a cover that literally (and paradoxically!) took my breath away. Your generosity of spirit is astounding. May the reach of your creativity be immense.

To Mike Burrows. Thank you for casting a professional eye over the design of this book and giving your hearty endorsement before it ever went to press.

To Chris and Kaye, Leonie, Lai Leng and Deb. People like you enable God's desires to become reality. We're all a team when it comes to getting a book like this across the line. Thank you for giving.

To God my Father. Thank you for owning me as your daughter when I was at my worst. The fact that I get to climb into Your embrace whenever I want speaks volumes about the restoration you brought me.

To Jesus. There was a time when I could call you my Saviour and nothing more. Now I know You as my Healer, my Deliverer, my Bridegroom, my Intercessor and my Friend. Thank You for not only taking my sins, but my sorrows as well. Learning to reign with You never grows old. I love You too.

To the Holy Spirit. It's no fun being un-Holy. Thank you for meeting me in my sin and sadness and getting me sorted from the inside out. Thank you for ministering comfort when the process got tough. For many years, I barely acknowledged You. Now, I love You. But more than that, I know You love me. Oh, and if progressive revelation is a spiritual love language, I'll take as much as You can give.

About the Author

Anya was born in New Zealand, moved to Australia as a child, and for thirty or so years has spanned many countries and cultures. She finished high school in Canada, was among the first wave of Christians to enter modern-day Albania, has ministered in the Czech Republic and more recently spent three years working alongside city officials, expat communities and Christian refugees in Turkey. With her husband, she has served in church planting and pastoral care, headed up prayer teams, taught seminars and discipleship groups, and with her innate love of people, has cultivated countless friendships along the way.

Anya's speaking and writing combine poignant story-telling, biblical richness, and a compelling call to personal wholeness and spiritual maturity. Her signature presentation '*The Story of the Daughter of Zion*' has been pivotal in women's lives around the world.

Anya lives in the Wellington region of New Zealand, where she and Jeff raise their four incredible children, develop Kingdom-focussed resources and nurture people in ministry. Anya loves nothing better than drinking a good cup of tea in the quiet early morning hours, preaching her heart out whether there's an audience or not, interacting with people from other cultures, and exploring the world with Jeff.

Torn Curtain Collective

Jeff and Anya McKee have together founded Torn Curtain Collective, a ministry that equips and empowers God's people to operate as confidently, naturally and effectively in the spiritual realm as they do in the physical.

To request Anya to speak at your church or event, email: connect@torncurtain.co.nz

To join the 'Feels Like I'm Breathing' online discussion group, head to: www.facebook.com/groups/feelslikeimbreathing

For more resources by Jeff and Anya, visit www.torncurtain.co.nz or follow us on instagram at torncurtaincollective